Best Easy Day Hikes Series

Best Easy Day Hikes
Olympic National Park

Second Edition

Erik Molvar

FALCONGUIDE

GUILFORD, CONNECTICUT
HELENA, MONTANA
AN IMPRINT OF THE GLOBE PEQUOT PRESS

FALCONGUIDES®

Maps created by Daniel Lloyd © Morris Book Publishing,
LLC.

Library of Congress Cataloging-in-Publication Data
Molvar, Erik.
  Best easy day hikes Olympic National Park / Erik
Molvar. – 2nd ed.
     p. cm.
  Rev. ed. of: Best easy day hikes, Olympics
  ISBN 978-0-7627-4120-5
  1. Hiking–Washington (State)–Olympic Mountains–
Guidebooks. 2. Trails–Washington (State)–Olympic
Mountains–Guidebooks. 3. Olympic Mountains (Wash.)–
Guidebooks. I. Molvar, Erik. Best easy day hikes,
Olympics. II. Title.
  GV199.42.W220486 2008
  917.97'940444–dc22

                                    2007042318
Printed in the United States of America
10 9 8 7 6 5 4 3 2

To buy books in quantity for corporate use
or incentives, call **(800) 962–0973**
or e-mail **premiums@GlobePequot.com**.

Contents

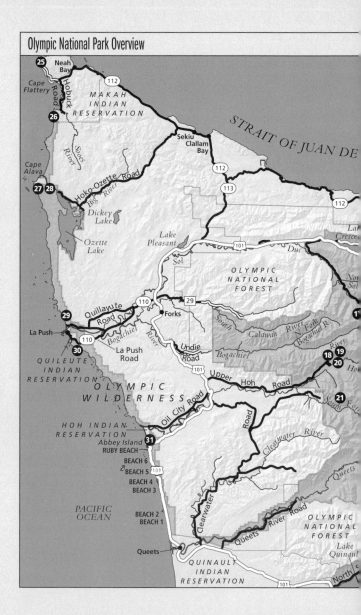

Olympic National Park Overview

STRAIT OF JUAN DE

Neah Bay
Cape Flattery
25
26

Hobuck Road

MAKAH INDIAN RESERVATION

112

Sekiu
Clallam Bay

112

113

112

Soos River

Cape Alava
27 **28**

Hoko-Ozette Road

Big River

Dickey Lake

Ozette Lake

Lake Pleasant

Sol

101

Duc

La Crescen

OLYMPIC NATIONAL FOREST

No Sol

1

Quillayute Road
110
29
Forks

29

South

Calawah River

N. Fork Bogachiel R.

18 **19**
20

River

29

La Push
110

Bogachiel River

La Push Road

Undie Road

Bogachiel

Ho

101

Upper   Hoh   Road

21

South Fo

QUILEUTE INDIAN RESERVATION

OLYMPIC WILDERNESS

Oil City Road

Road

Cleatwater River

HOH INDIAN RESERVATION

Abbey Island
31
RUBY BEACH
BEACH 6
BEACH 5
BEACH 4
BEACH 3

101

River

Queets

BEACH 2
BEACH 1

PACIFIC OCEAN

Cleatwater

Queets   River   Road

OLYMPIC NATIONAL FOREST

Lake Quinault

Queets

QUINAULT INDIAN RESERVATION

101

North

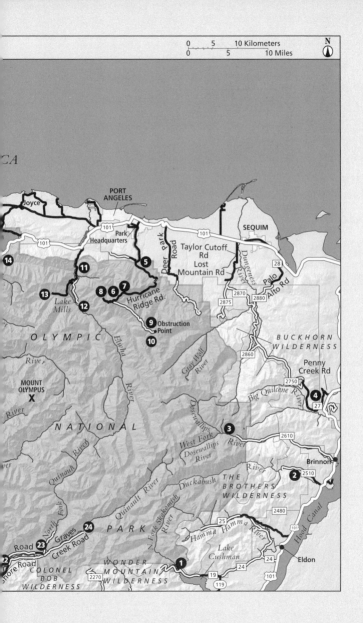

0   5   10 Kilometers

0   5   10 Miles

N

CA

Joyce

PORT ANGELES

101

Park Headquarters

SEQUIM

101

Taylor Cutoff Rd

Lost Mountain Rd

28

5

14

101

Deer Park Road

Dungeness River

Palo Alto Rd

11

13

8 **6** **7**

Hurricane Ridge Rd.

2870

2875

2880

Lake Mills

12

9 Obstruction Point

10

2860

BUCKHORN WILDERNESS

O L Y M P I C

River

Elwha

River

Gray Wolf River

Penny Creek Rd

2750

MOUNT OLYMPUS
X

River

N A T I O N A L

River

Quinault River

Dosewallips

River

Big Quilcene River

4

27

3

West Fork Dosewallips River

River

2610

Brinnon

North Fork

Quinault River

Duckabush River

T H E
B R O T H E R S
W I L D E R N E S S

2

2510

2480

River

Graves

Creek Road

24

P A R K

N. Fork Skokomish River

25

Hamma Hamma River

101

24

23

Shore Road

Road

2

C O L O N E L
B O B
W I L D E R N E S S

W O N D E R
M O U N T A I N
W I L D E R N E S S

2270

Lake Cushman

1

19

119

24

101

Hood Canal

Eldon

Acknowledgments

Thanks to Bill Baccus and Ruth Scott for providing information and reviewing this book. The introductory material is largely the work of Bill Schneider. Special thanks to my wife, Melanie, for providing good company during the field research.

Help Us Keep This Guide Up to Date

Every effort has been made by the author and editors to make this guide as accurate and useful as possible. However, many things can change after a guide is published—trails are rerouted, regulations change, techniques evolve, facilities come under new management, etc.

We would love to hear from you concerning your experiences with this guide and how you feel it could be improved and kept up to date. While we may not be able to respond to all comments and suggestions, we'll take them to heart and we'll also make certain to share them with the author. Please send your comments and suggestions to the following address:

The Globe Pequot Press
Reader Response/Editorial Department
P.O. Box 480
Guilford, CT 06437

Or you may e-mail us at:

editorial@GlobePequot.com

Thanks for your input, and happy trails!

Introduction

What's a "best easy" hike?

Our national parks and forests serve as windows to the natural world, reservoirs of natural beauty and grandeur, and wellsprings on inspiration. As such, they are magnets to people who seek to reestablish their ties with nature, learn more about the world in which we live, or simply find a quiet escape from the hustle and bustle of modern society. Olympic National Park features mountain fastnesses clad in glaciers, mysterious rain forests, and a wild and rugged coastline, inviting the visitor to step into the natural world.

Anyone who travels widely in these areas will soon notice that there are two distinct categories of visitors—those who want to immerse themselves in the wilderness of Olympic National Park for several days at a time, and those who only have a day or two and would like a choice sampling of the special features of the area. This book is for the second group.

The materials for this guide were gathered as I researched the much larger and more comprehensive book, *Hiking Olympic National Park*. That larger book covers many trails in the park and the surrounding areas and every coastal hiking route, including those that are neither best nor easy. *Best Easy Day Hikes Olympic National Park* includes only short, less strenuous hikes that showcase the best features of the Olympic Peninsula.

These hikes vary in length, but most are short (less than 5 miles). Most lack big hills, and those few long grades that appear in this book are tackled in a leisurely fashion. All hikes are on easy-to-follow trails and beaches with no route-finding challenges. Trailhead access is easy for all hikes, and you can reach any of these trailheads with a low-clearance passenger car.

Some of the hikes in this book might seem easy to some but more difficult to others. To help you decide, I've ranked the hikes from easiest to most challenging. Please keep in mind that long does not always equal difficult. Other factors, such as elevation gain and trail conditions, have to be considered.

I hope you thoroughly enjoy your "best easy" hiking through the natural wonders of Olympic National Park.

Ranking the Hikes

The following list ranks the hikes in this book from easiest to most challenging.

Madison Creek Falls
Sol Duc Falls
Maple Glade Nature Trail
Ranger Hole
Spruce Nature Trail
Hoh River
Lover's Lane
Hall of Mosses Nature Trail
Cascading Terraces Nature Trail
Hole-in-the-Wall
Hurricane Ridge Loops
The Spruce Railroad Trail
Staircase Rapids
Hurricane Hill
Marymere Falls
Irely Lake
Ruby Beach
Cape Flattery
The Quillayute Needles
Cape Alava
Sand Point
Olympic Hot Springs
Heart o' the Forest Trail
West Fork Dosewallips Gorge
The South Fork of the Hoh River
Lillian Ridge
Geyser Valley Loop

Shi Shi Beach
Mount Angeles
Elk Mountain
Mount Zion

Zero Impact

Traveling in a national park such as Olympic is like visiting a famous museum. You obviously don't want to leave your mark on an art treasure in the museum. If everybody who visited the museum left one tiny mark, the piece of art would be destroyed—and what would a big building full of trashed art be worth? The same goes for pristine wilderness like that found in Olympic National Park. If we all left just one little mark on the landscape, the wilderness would soon be despoiled.

A wilderness can accommodate plenty of human use as long as everybody treats it with respect. But a few thoughtless or uninformed visitors can ruin it for everyone who follows. And the need for good manners applies to all wilderness visitors, not just backpackers. Day hikers should also adhere strictly to the "zero impact" principles. The book *Leave No Trace* is a valuable resource for learning more about these principles (ordering information in back of this book).

Three FalconGuides Principles of Zero Impact

- Leave with everything you brought with you.
- Leave no sign of your visit.
- Leave the landscape as you found it.

Most of us know better than to litter—in or out of the wilderness. Even the tiniest scrap of paper left along the trail or at the campsite detracts from the pristine character of the Olympic landscape. This means that you should pack out everything, even biodegradable items such as orange peels, which can take years to decompose. It's also a good idea to pick up any trash that less considerate hikers have left behind.

To avoid damaging the trailside soil and plants, stay on the main path. Avoid cutting switchbacks and venturing onto fragile vegetation. When hiking on trailless beaches, stick to unvegetated surfaces below the storm tide mark, and don't disturb the fragile animals in tide pools. When taking a rest stop, select a durable surface like a bare log, a rock, or a sandy beach.

Don't pick up "souvenirs," such as rocks, antlers, feathers, or wildflowers. The next person wants to discover them, too, and taking such souvenirs violates park regulations.

Avoid making loud noises that disturb the silence that others may be enjoying. Remember, sound travels easily in the outdoors. Be courteous.

When nature calls, use established outhouse facilities whenever possible. If these are unavailable, bury human waste 6 to 8 inches deep and pack out used toilet paper. This is a good reason to carry a lightweight trowel. Keep wastes at least 300 feet away from any surface water or boggy spots.

Finally, and perhaps most important, strictly follow the pack-it-in/pack-it-out rule. If you carry something into the wilderness, consume it completely or carry it out with you.

Make zero impact—put your ear to the ground in the wilderness and listen carefully. Thousands of people coming behind you are thanking you for your courtesy and good sense.

LEGEND

═══════	Interstate Highway
═══════	Paved Road
- - - - - -	Unpaved Road
⑤	Interstate Highway
④	State Road
②	US Highway
▬▬▬▬▬	National Park Boundary
▬▬▬▬▬	National Forest Boundary
───────	State Boundary
───────	River
───────	Creek
▬ ▬ ▬ ▬	Featured Trail
– – – –	Other Trail
···········	Trailless Route
◯	Glacier
X^{7524}	Mountain Peak
Λ	Campsite
▲	Ranger Station
⌐⌐	Pass/Saddle
▪	Building
178	Forest Road
➊—	Start
◯	Trailhead
⌇	Spring
⊙	Overlook
✚	Coastal Beach Marker
⌇	Falls

The Leeward Olympics

This region of the park lies on the leeward side of the Olympic Mountains. Prevailing winds from the southwest are pushed upward because of the mountains, and the air dumps its moisture on the western slopes as it cools. Little moisture remains for the northeastern corner of the range, which is known as a "rainshadow" area. The geology and ecology of the rain shadow is defined in many ways by this lack of precipitation. Glaciers that buried the central mountains during the last ice age filled only the valleys here, and the rounded ridgetops became refuges for alpine plants and animals amid a sea of glacial ice. An astonishing diversity of wildflowers can be found here to this day, occupying habitats that range from alpine tundra to semidesert.

Farther south, an abundance of short rivers penetrates the rugged outer ranges of the Olympic Mountains on their way to Hood Canal, a branch of Puget Sound. These rivers offer travel corridors into the interior of the park, where a high alpine country of rugged, glacier-clad peaks is interspersed with lush meadows filled with wildflowers. The climate here is a transition between the temperate rain forests of the west and the rain shadow forests of the northeast. Valley bottoms harbor a lush growth of vegetation, while the nearby slopes may have dry montane forests. Lake Cushman, which lies outside the park on private lands, is a prime attraction of the area. Its close proximity to Seattle translates into weekend crowds when the weather is sunny.

The interior of the region falls within Olympic National Park, while the outer ranges and foothills are managed by the Forest Service. There is a Forest Service visitor center in Quilcene. Smaller National Park Service ranger stations are staffed during the summer at Staircase and on the Dosewallips River.

There are Forest Service campgrounds on the Dosewallips, Duckabush, and Hamma Hamma Rivers, and also at Big Creek and Lilliwaup Creek. In Olympic National Park there are campgrounds at Staircase and on the Dosewallips River, while the state of Washington maintains heavily developed campgrounds at Dosewallips and Lake Cushman State Parks. Some services and facilities can be found along U.S. Highway 101 in the villages of Hoodsport, Eldon, and Brinnon. A wider array of services can be found at Quilcene.

1 Staircase Rapids

Type of hike: Out-and-back.
Total distance: 2 miles round-trip.
Elevation change: 200-foot gain, 200-foot loss.

Approximate hiking time: 1 to 2 hours.
Topo maps: USGS Mount Steel; Custom Correct *Mount Skokomish–Lake Cushman.*

Finding the trailhead: From Hoodsport, drive west on Lake Cushman Road past Lake Cushman State Park. Turn left onto Forest Road 24 and drive 6.6 miles to the Staircase Ranger Station. The hike begins at the Staircase Rapids Trailhead, across the auto bridge from the ranger station.

The Hike

A popular footpath follows the south bank of the Skokomish River's North Fork, passing foaming white water and deep pools on the river. The footbridge that used to span the river at mile 1 has been washed out by flooding, interrupting a former loop hike. Regardless, this is a great hike for folks who wish to view old-growth trees as well as the crystalline pools and rushing rapids on one of the major rivers of the Olympic Peninsula.

The hike begins near the Staircase Ranger Station, just across the bridge at the edge of an open meadow. The well-beaten trail parallels the river as it moves upward through the conifers and vine maples. Early in the hike, a spur path accesses a western red cedar that is more than 14 feet in diameter. The main trail wanders toward the riverbank, making periodic visits to the rapids for pleasant views of the rushing water and crystalline pools. After 0.6 mile a spur

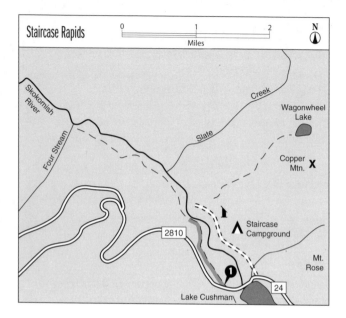

0   1   2   N

Miles

Skokomish River

Four Stream

Creek

Slate

Wagonwheel Lake

Copper Mtn. **X**

2810

Staircase Campground

Mt. Rose

24

Lake Cushman

path accesses a hole known locally as "Red Reef Pool." Here the river has cut a channel through a shelf of limestone that is tinted red with oxidized iron. The water plunges over the shelf, then roils in the aquamarine depths of the pool. A little farther on, a second spur descends to "Dolly Varden Pool," its depths punctuated by enormous boulders.

The main trail continues upstream beside Staircase Rapids to reach the former site of the footbridge. The trail upriver to Four Stream has been abandoned farther upstream; retrace your steps to complete the hike.

Key Points

0.0 Staircase Rapids Trailhead, south bank of North Fork Skokomish River.

0.2 Spur trail runs north to large western red cedar.

0.6 Spur trail to "Red Reef Pool."

0.7 Spur trail to "Dolly Varden Pool."

0.8 Junction with trail to Four Stream.

1.0 Hike ends at old bridge site.

2.0 Return to traihead.

2 Ranger Hole

Type of hike: Out-and-back.
Total distance: 1.7 miles round-trip.
Elevation change: Minimal.

Approximate hiking time: 45 minutes to 1.5 hours.
Topo maps: USGS Mount Jupiter; Custom Correct *The Brothers–Mount Anderson.*

Finding the trailhead: From Brinnon, drive south on U.S. Highway 101 to milepost 310. Turn west onto Duckabush Road (Forest Road 2510) and drive 3.9 miles to the marked trailhead.

The Hike

The trail begins at the historic Interrorem Ranger Station. This tightly built log cabin with its distinctive pyramidal roof served as the original ranger headquarters for Mount Olympus National Monument, which was to become a national park in 1938. A self-guided nature trail of 0.2 mile loops through the forest behind the cabin, which has grown in the wake of logging that dates from the mid-1800s. Walk the

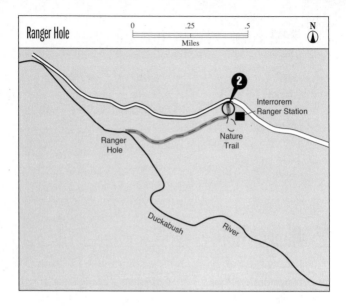

interpretive trail as a prelude, and you will be able to identify the plants of the lowland forest community.

The Ranger Hole Trail begins by winding southwest through a second-growth forest. It passes a modern clear-cut before dropping sharply to reach the banks of the Duckabush River after 0.8 mile. Here the river charts a foaming passage through a narrow slot in the bedrock, then spreads out into the placid and crystalline depths of Ranger Hole. Steelhead could once be seen holding in the depths of this pool during their spawning migration. Siltation from clearcutting has since buried their spawning gravels in muck, and the adult steelhead population has been depleted by heavy fishing pressure.

Turn around here to complete the hike.

3 West Fork Dosewallips Gorge

Type of hike: Out-and-back.
Total distance: 4.8 miles round-trip.
Elevation change: 530-foot gain.
Approximate hiking time: 2.5 to 4 hours.
Topo maps: USGS The Brothers; Custom Correct *The Brothers–Mount Anderson.*

Finding the trailhead: From mile 306.1 on U.S. Highway 101 in the north part of Brinnon, turn west onto Dosewallips Road (Forest Road 2610). Drive 15.5 miles to the trailhead at road's end.

The Hike

This hike visits the forested lowlands of the Dosewallips River (pronounced "doh-see-WAH-lups"). This river is fed by melting glaciers, and the fine silt ground up by the glaciers has turned the water a translucent turquoise color. In addition to views of the water at Dose Forks Camp and the deep canyon of the West Fork, visitors will enjoy the silent grandeur of a climax coniferous forest.

Begin the trek by climbing the hillside beyond the Dosewallips Ranger Station. The Dose Terrace Trail soon loops away to the left, running along the riverbank only to return to the main trail 0.4 mile farther on. Meanwhile the Dosewallips Trail climbs through a mature forest of tall, slender hemlock and Douglas fir. After crossing Pass Creek, the climbing eases, and the surrounding ridges can be seen through gaps in the thinning canopy. The trail crosses a second woodland stream before reaching a major junction. After 1.4 miles the trail reaches a major fork: The West Fork Trail that runs to the Dose Forks camping area and on to

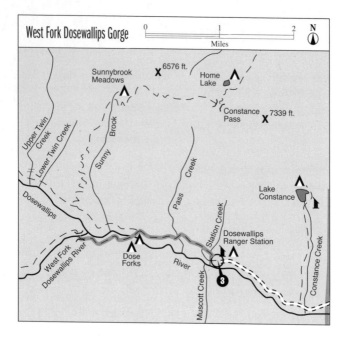

West Fork Dosewallips Gorge

```
0          1          2    N
|_____|_____|    ⬤
        Miles
```

Upper Twin Creek
Lower Twin Creek
Dosewallips
Sunnybrook Meadows
Sunny Brook
X 6576 ft.
Home Lake
Constance Pass
X 7339 ft.
Pass Creek
Lake Constance
Station Creek
Dosewallips Ranger Station
Constance Creek
Dose Forks
West Fork Dosewallips River
River
Muscott Creek
❸

Anderson Pass drops down to the left, while the Dosewallips Trail ascends to the right.

Turn left onto the West Fork Trail, which immediately descends to the Dose Forks Camp. The tent sites are set amid a grove of immense Douglas firs beside the swirling turquoise waters of the Dosewallips. Just beyond the camp is a sturdy bridge to the south bank of the river. Once there, the trail ascends briskly onto forested slopes high above the water.

The actual "forks" of the Dosewallips lie 0.6 mile above the camp, and the trail skirts to the edge of a steep bluff to overlook the converging waters of the west and main forks of the Dosewallips River. A second bridge spans the deep chasm of the West Fork, and the waters churn through a turbulent passage far below it. On the canyon rims, a dry forest of western hemlock is underlain by a sparse growth of salal. Pacific rhododendrons are abundant here; watch for their pink blossoms in May. There are no restraining structures along the lip of the gorge; stay well away from the edge and use the bridge to view the chasm. Return to the trailhead via the same route.

Key Points

0.0   Trailhead.

0.1   First junction with Dosewallips Terrace Trail. Stay right.

0.5   Second junction with Dosewallips Terrace Trail. Stay right.

1.4   Junction with Anderson Pass Trail. Turn left.

1.6   Dose Forks Camp. Trail crosses Dosewallips River.

2.4   Bridge spans the chasm of West Fork of the Dosewallips.

4.8   Return to the trailhead.

4   Mount Zion

Type of hike: Out-and-back.
Total distance: 3.6 miles round-trip.
Elevation change: 1,340-foot gain.

Approximate hiking time: 2 to 4 hours.
Topo maps: USGS Mount Zion; Custom Correct *Buckhorn Wilderness.*

Finding the trailhead: From Sequim, drive east on U.S. Highway 101 to mile 267.4 and turn south onto Palo Alto Road. The pavement ends after 6 miles, and the road becomes Forest Road 28. Drive another 7 miles or so to Forest Road 2810. Turn left and follow this secondary road 2 miles to the marked trailhead. From Quilcene,

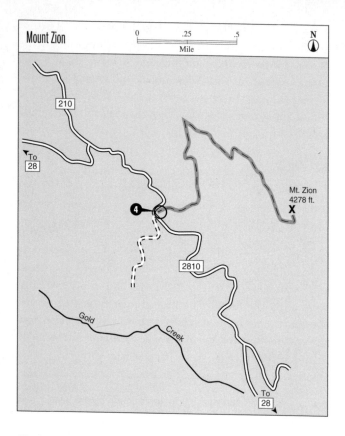

Mount Zion

0   .25   .5
Mile

N

210

To 28

4

Mt. Zion
4278 ft.
X

2810

Gold Creek

To 28

drive north on US 101 to the Lords Lake Loop Road. Follow this road to FR 28, then drive northwest on this trunk road to reach the junction with FR 2810 at Bon Jon Pass. Turn right and follow FR 2810 the remaining 2 miles to the trailhead.

The Hike

This trail offers one of the easiest ascents to a summit in the Olympic Mountains. From its position at the leeward edge of the mountains, views stretch across the glittering waters of Puget Sound to the snowy crags of the Cascade Range, with its dormant volcanoes rising high above glacier-carved ridges. The trail does not offer a wilderness setting; Mount Zion lies within the Olympic National Forest and is surrounded by clear-cuts. Hikers may have to share the trail with motorbikes (although the narrow trail and bumpy water bars discourage most dirt bikers). The trail is especially spectacular in early July, when the pink blossoms of Pacific rhododendron light up the forests that skirt the peak.

The trail begins by following a forested finger ridge to the base of the mountain, then climbs steadily across the slopes on a northerly heading. The large, shiny leaves of the rhododendron crowd the forest understory in these early stretches, and it is here that the best displays of blossoms are to be found. The trail ultimately doglegs to the southeast, climbing beneath basalt monoliths that rise from the wooded slopes. One of the tallest outcrops yields westward views of Gray Wolf Ridge, capped by a row of impressive peaks.

Just below the summit, the trail embarks upon a series of tight switchbacks. The trail ends in a grassy clearing on the mountaintop. While views of the Olympic Mountains are screened by the trees, a broad panorama of Puget Sound stretches below. To the northeast, the snowy cone of Mount Baker and its smaller neighbor, Mount Shuksan, rise beyond Discovery and Sequim Bays. Far to the southeast, Mount Rainier soars skyward, its glistening glaciers dwarfing the wooded ridges that surround it. Retrace the trail back to the trailhead to complete the hike.

Key Points

0.0   Mount Zion Trailhead.

0.7   Trail reaches overlook rock.

1.8   Summit of Mount Zion.

3.6   Return to the trailhead.

Hurricane Ridge

Extremely popular with day hikers, the high alpine meadows of Hurricane Ridge are easily reached from Port Angeles via a paved road. The entire length of Hurricane Ridge from Obstruction Point to Hurricane Hill escaped glaciation during the ice ages, serving as a refuge for alpine plants and animals. The result is an outstanding diversity of wildflowers, featuring several species that are found nowhere else in the world. There are excellent opportunities for wildlife viewing, particularly black-tailed deer and Olympic marmots, in the extensive alpine meadows.

The main visitor center for Olympic National Park is located at the beginning of Hurricane Ridge Road at the southern edge of Port Angeles. A smaller visitor center is sited in the meadows atop Hurricane Ridge, and ranger-guided interpretive walks are organized from this point. The more primitive Obstruction Point Road, a narrow gravel road with pullouts that is not suited to motor homes or trailers but can be negotiated by most passenger cars, departs near this point. This road is cleared of snow in July and closes at the end of September. Deer Park Road is a similar gravel trunk road that climbs steeply from the coastal plains east of Port Angeles to the mountaintops. There are auto campgrounds at Deer Park as well as Heart o' the Hills, which is just inside the park boundary on Hurricane Ridge Road. All services can be found in the towns of Port Angeles and Sequim.

5 Heart o' the Forest Trail

Type of hike: Out-and-back.
Total distance: 4.1 miles round-trip.
Elevation change: 200-foot loss.

Approximate hiking time: 2 to 3.5 hours.
Topo maps: USGS Port Angeles; Custom Correct *Hurricane Ridge*.

Finding the trailhead: From the park visitor center in Port Angeles, drive 6.4 miles up Hurricane Ridge Road to the Heart o' the Hills Campground. The trail begins from a marked trailhead on Campground Loop E.

The Hike

This approximately 2-mile trail leads into the forest to the east of the Heart o' the Hills Campground. It offers no mountain views, but does travel through some of the most stately old-growth forest on the Olympic Peninsula. This ancient woodland is made up of silver fir, red cedar, and Douglas fir, with some of the largest trees exceeding 8 feet in diameter. Old trees often die from the top down, and the broken-topped giants provide the unique nesting habitat for the northern spotted owl, one of the most celebrated and controversial of our endangered species.

The trail stays fairly level for the majority of its length, where numerous rills are choked with the giant leaves of devil's club and skunk cabbage. As the widely spaced giants give way to a younger stand of hemlock and Douglas fir, the

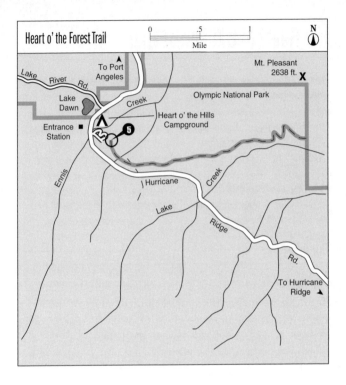

path descends steadily into a narrow creek valley. The trail ends rather ignominiously at the park boundary, where the forest has been clear-cut right up to the edge of the park, swallowing up the trail in the process. Turn around here to complete the hike.

Big Meadow Loop

6 Hurricane Ridge Loops

Type of hike: A series of loops.
Total distance: 0.3 mile to 1.5 miles, depending on route.
Elevation change: Minimal to 200-foot gain, depending on route.

Approximate hiking time: 20 minutes to 1.5 hours, depending on route.
Topo maps: USGS Mount Angeles; Custom Correct *Hurricane Ridge*.

Finding the trailhead: From Port Angeles, drive 17.6 miles south on Hurricane Ridge Road to the visitor center atop the ridge. The trails depart from the northeast corner of the parking lot.

The Hikes

A network of walking trails wanders through the subalpine meadows atop Hurricane Ridge. This popular area receives more visitors than any other spot within the park, and because of the heavy foot traffic, most of the trails have been paved. The sole exception is the High Ridge Loop, which is graveled and has a more challenging grade than the other trails, which are quite easy. All of the trails offer outstanding views of the mountains, including Mount Olympus when the weather cooperates. A startling diversity of wildflowers offers a different combination of blossoms with each passing week. Mule deer and Olympic marmots are abundant here, and they are unafraid of humans. (Do not feed them!) There is a visitor center across the parking lot, and guided ranger walks are offered on a periodic basis. Each trail within the network will be discussed separately. The author's favorite routing follows the Cirque Rim Trail, with a side trip up the High Ridge Loop for an overall hike of 1.3 miles.

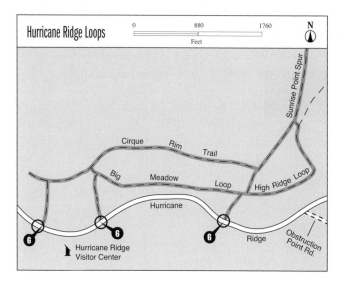

Big Meadow Loop: This short loop wanders through the lush meadows beside the parking lot. Though crowded, this trail offers the best opportunities to view wildlife and alpine flowers. A broad panorama of the Olympic Mountains spans the horizon to the south.

Cirque Rim Trail: This trail follows the northern edge of Hurricane Ridge, passing through copses of subalpine fir and secluded glades. A spur path descends from its westernmost point to reach an overlook of the Little River valley, which is guarded by Hurricane Hill, Unicorn Peak, and Griff Peak. As the main trail follows the rim of a glacial cirque, openings reveal northward vistas that encompass the Strait of Juan de Fuca and Vancouver Island rising beyond it. During clear weather, both Port Angeles and Victoria, British Columbia, are visible. Mount Angeles is the prominent summit to the east, while below the trail is a ski lift that serves cross-country skiers during the winter months. Upon reaching it, the Cirque Rim Trail turns south; follow it downward through the meadows to return to the parking lot.

High Ridge Loop: This 0.5-mile hike begins at the northeast corner of the Big Meadow Loop and ascends a steep ridgeline. It soon reaches a level overlook that commands excellent views. The Lillian River valley stretches southward, far below, with snow-dappled peaks on both sides. The next valley to the west bears the Elwha River, and beyond it are the Bailey Range and Mount Olympus itself. The pavement ends here, and now a gravel walkway completes the moderate ascent to the crest of a rocky knoll. The path then descends to a junction with the Sunrise Point and Mount Angeles Trails (the latter is a longer trek—see the Mount Angeles hike description). Take a hard left to continue the loop hike, which descends rather steeply through a subalpine woodland. Turn left at the top of the ski lift, where a paved path leads across the Big Meadow Loop and back to the parking lot.

Sunrise Point Spur: This short side path ascends from the High Ridge Trail to the top of a stony knob. With a little jockeying for position, one can have views in all directions, featuring the Bailey Range and Mount Olympus to the southwest, Unicorn Peak to the west, and Steeple Rock to the southeast, with the broad and snowy massif of Elk Mountain beyond it.

7 Mount Angeles

Type of hike: Shuttle.
Total distance: 3.4 miles one way.
Elevation change: 520-foot gain, 1,320-foot loss.

Approximate hiking time: 1.5 to 3 hours.
Topo maps: USGS Mount Angeles; Custom Correct *Hurricane Ridge.*

Finding the trailhead: From Port Angeles, drive 17.6 miles south on Hurricane Ridge Road to the visitor center atop the ridge. The hike begins on the High Ridge Trail, which departs from the northeast corner of the parking lot. The trail ends at the Switchback Trailhead (also known as the Third Peak parking area), 3 miles down Hurricane Ridge Road from the Hurricane Ridge Visitor Center.

The Hike

This hike begins in the tourist-thronged meadows atop Hurricane Ridge, but the crowds thin out abruptly as the trail ventures eastward through the spectacular meadows on the shoulders of Klahhane Ridge. Virtually the entire trek is at or above timberline, and wildflower displays are often impressive. Superb vistas encompass the heart of the Olympic Mountains, with the glacier-clad summit of Mount Olympus presiding above the lesser crags.

The trip begins in the complex of paved nature trails on Hurricane Ridge. Follow the High Ridge Trail northeastward as it climbs through alpine meadows. The junction with the Mount Angeles Trail is just beyond the first knob on the ridgetop. This path rises and falls, tracking the ridgetop northeastward through alpine meadows interrupted by stands of perfectly conical subalpine firs. There are

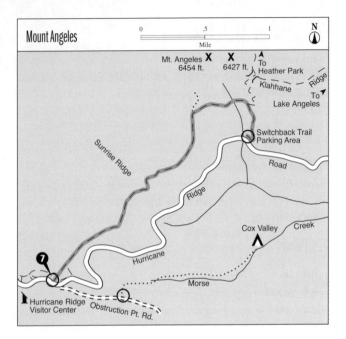

wildflowers of all varieties here, highlighted by lupines, lark-spurs, bistorts, and a magenta variety of paintbrush that is endemic to the Olympics. To the south lies a sea of snow-capped peaks. The rugged Bailey Range partially screens Mount Olympus to the southwest, while Steeple Rock rises in front of Elk Mountain farther east.

When the trail reaches the base of Mount Angeles, an unmarked climber's trail shoots straight up toward the summit. Bear right as the main trail runs beneath the twisted basalt spires that guard the flanks of the peak. The path soon makes a shallow descent to intercept the Switchback Trail.

Dedicated hikers will want to climb up to the saddle in Klahhane Ridge, which overlooks a nameless basin guarded by rugged ridges. (This fairly strenuous side trip adds 1.9 miles to the length of the trek.) There is a good possibility of sighting marmots and chipmunks on the ridgetop. More rarely, mountain goats and black bears are spotted in the basin or among the rocks above it. Hardy alpine plants like spreading phlox and creeping penstemon brighten the rockscape.

Visitors who are pressed for time can hike directly down the Switchback Trail to regain the road far below the starting point. A foot-pounding series of switchbacks leads down the mountainside, passing copses of fir and mountain hemlock en route to the Third Peak parking area.

Key Points

- **0.0** Hurricane Ridge parking area.
- **0.4** Mount Angeles Trail departs from High Ridge Trail.
- **2.2** Way trail toward summit. Bear right.
- **2.7** Junction with Switchback Trail. Turn right to begin descent.
- **3.4** Trail reaches Hurricane Ridge Road at Switchback Trail parking area, where you retrieve your car or are picked up.

8 Hurricane Hill

Type of hike: Out-and-back.
Total distance: 2.9 miles round-trip.
Elevation change: 660-foot gain.

Approximate hiking time: 1.5 to 3 hours.
Topo maps: USGS Hurricane Hill; Custom Correct *Hurricane Ridge*.

Finding the trailhead: From Port Angeles, drive south 18.9 miles on Hurricane Ridge Road. The hike begins at the road's end, where a parking area marks the trailhead.

The Hike

This trail offers a scenic walk to a grassy summit at the western end of Hurricane Ridge. Most tourists never get farther than the Hurricane Ridge Visitor Center; if you take the extra drive out to Hurricane Hill, you can enjoy the same beautiful meadows, mountain wildlife, and spectacular vistas without the crowds. This route follows a paved nature trail with interpretive plaques, and though it does have some ups and downs, it is wheelchair accessible for the first half mile.

The hike begins with a gradual climb along a flower-strewn ridgeline. There are outstanding views of the Bailey Range here, and black-tailed deer and Olympic marmots are sometimes sighted. The trail soon reaches a saddle where the stark and forbidding heights of Mount Angeles can be seen to the east. The Little River Trail drops from this low pass into the valley to the north. The main path continues to climb the grassy flanks of Hurricane Hill, reaching a second junction near the top. To the right, the paved trail runs 0.1 mile to the summit of the hill, which overlooks a shallow alpine tarn and provides good views of Unicorn Peak. The broader panorama encompasses the Strait of Juan de Fuca and Canada to the

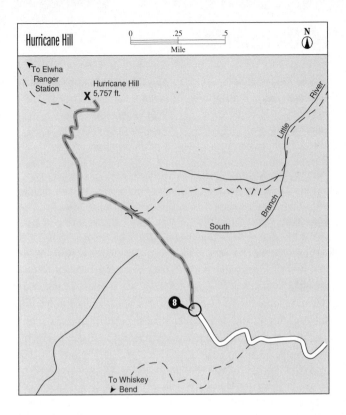

To Elwha
Ranger
Station

Hurricane Hill
X 5,757 ft.

Little River

Branch

South

8

To Whiskey
► Bend

north and the regal summit of Mount Olympus to the south.
Turn around here to complete the hike.

Key Points

- **0.0** Trailhead.
- **0.4** Junction with Little River Trail. Keep going straight.
- **1.4** Spur trail to summit of Hurricane Hill.
- **1.5** Summit of Hurricane Hill.
- **2.9** Return to the trailhead.

9 Elk Mountain

Type of hike: Shuttle.
Total distance: 7.4 miles one way.
Elevation change: 1,260-foot gain, 2,120-foot loss.

Approximate hiking time: 4 to 7 hours.
Topo maps: USGS Mount Angeles; Custom Correct *Gray Wolf–Dosewallips.*

Finding the trailhead: From Port Angeles, drive 17.6 miles south on Hurricane Ridge Road to the visitor center parking lot. Turn sharply left (south) onto the narrow, winding Obstruction Point Road. This route is too narrow for trailers and RVs. Drive 7.6 miles to the road's end at Obstruction Point. The trail begins at the north end of the parking area. The hike ends at the ranger station at Deer Park.

The Hike

This trail offers a point-to-point hike across alpine ridges from Obstruction Point in the west to the Deer Park Campground in the east. Water is scarce along this route, so be sure to bring along a plentiful supply. A steep snowfield may block the beginning of the Elk Mountain Trail. An ice ax may be required before mid-July.

The trail begins by crossing a grassy bowl that is home to a marmot colony; the engaging behavior of these social rodents can entertain you for hours. The path drops across the steep headwall of the Badger Valley as it rounds Obstruction Peak, and the Badger Valley Trail drops away to the right. Continue straight on the Elk Mountain Trail. The path then begins to ascend onto the broad summit of Elk Mountain, with its endless rocky fells sprinkled with the blossoms of phlox and dwarf lupine. The rocky interstices support a

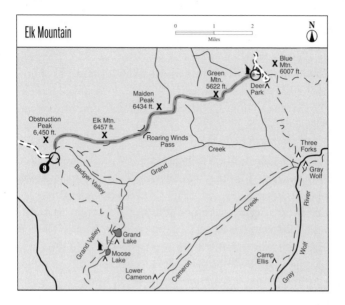

0   1   2
Miles

N

Blue
Mtn.
X 6007 ft.

Green
Mtn.
5622 ft. X

Deer
Park

Maiden
Peak
6434 ft. X

Obstruction
Peak
6,450 ft.
X

Elk Mtn.
6457 ft.
X

Roaring Winds
Pass

Creek

Three
Forks

Gray
Wolf

Badger Valley

Grand

Creek

River

Grand Valley

Grand
Lake

Moose
Lake

Camp
Ellis

Lower
Cameron

Cameron

Gray

Wolf

9

sparse growth of hardy lichens that are close cousins to the
ones that provide Arctic caribou herds with their winter for-
age. Take a glance backward for a grandstand view of the
heart of the Olympic Mountains, from Mount Christie in
the south to the Bailey Range in the north, and surmounted
by the ice-bound mass of Mount Olympus itself. To the
south, the glacier-clad summit of Mount Cameron is partially hidden by the ridges that rise above the Grand Valley.
The ragged spires of the Needles rise farther to the east.

As Elk Mountain peters out, the trail descends steeply to
reach Roaring Winds Pass. The trail then climbs high onto
the flanks of Maiden Peak. The south slope of this peak is
quite arid and supports a rather sparse flora of grasses and
lichens interspersed with bistorts and dwarf lupines. A short

trek to the ridgeline allows the traveler to look down into the basin containing Maiden Lake, a small, shallow pool of pale aquamarine. The slopes of Maiden Peak offer the park's finest view of the Needles, which are, from north to south, Mount Walkinshaw, Mount Clark, and Mount Johnson. Mount Deception is the southernmost summit on this craggy ridge.

The path rounds the rocky eastern spur of Maiden Peak, then descends through rolling tundra as subalpine firs close in around the ridgeline. Moist glades support white and pink heathers, avalanche lilies, and a deep lavender variety of paintbrush. As the trail drops onto the south slope of Green Mountain, it enters an arid forest of lodgepole pine. There is little in the way of understory vegetation here, and this habitat type is avoided by most species of wildlife. After a rather long and jolting descent into a low saddle, the trail picks up an old roadbed that climbs the remaining distance to reach the hike's end at the Deer Park Ranger Station. Hikers who do not have a vehicle waiting should turn around here to complete the hike.

Key Points

- **0.0**   Obstruction Point Trailhead.
- **0.2**   Junction with Badger Valley Trail. Keep going straight.
- **2.0**   Junction with cutoff trail to Badger Valley. Bear left.
- **2.6**   Easternmost summit of Elk Mountain.
- **3.2**   Roaring Winds Pass.
- **3.9**   Maiden Peak.
- **7.4**   Deer Park Ranger Station and your vehicle or a ride.

10 **Lillian Ridge**

Type of hike: Out-and-back.
Total distance: 3.2 miles round-trip.
Elevation change: 510-foot gain, 170-foot loss to turnaround point.

Approximate hiking time: 1.5 to 3 hours.
Topo maps: USGS Mount Angeles; Custom Correct *Gray Wolf–Dosewallips.*

Finding the trailhead: From Port Angeles, drive 17.6 miles south on Hurricane Ridge Road to the visitor center parking lot. Turn sharply left (south) onto the narrow, winding Obstruction Point Road. This route is too narrow for trailers and RVs. Drive 7.6 miles to the road's end at Obstruction Point. The trail runs south from the parking area.

The Hike

This outstanding ridge trek follows Lillian Ridge, an alpine divide that offers views of sparkling lakes and a broad sweep of the eastern Olympics.

The trail begins at Obstruction Point, where a colony of marmots has excavated a network of tunnels. Their playful antics are on display for anyone who can remain inconspicuous for a while. The trail soon climbs onto the rounded top of Lillian Ridge, clad in lush meadows that grade into an arid alpine tundra. This is an alpine desert in which hardy flowers such as dwarf lupine, phlox, and fleabane eke out a hardscrabble existence in the gusting winds, short growing seasons, and lack of water found here. Spectacular scenery stretches in all directions. To the east, the Needles rise sheer above the intervening ridgetops. To the south, McCartney Peak rises above the Lillian River valley amid a sea of equally

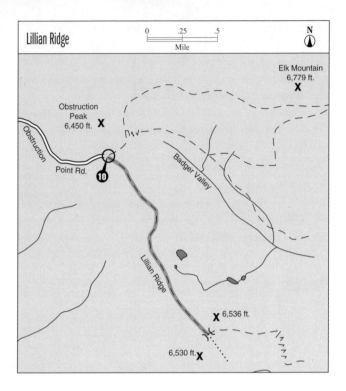

Lillian Ridge

0   .25   .5
Mile

N

Elk Mountain
6,779 ft.
X

Obstruction
Peak
6,450 ft. X

Obstruction

Point Rd.

10

Badger Valley

Lillian Ridge

X 6,536 ft.

6,530 ft. X

spectacular (though nameless) summits, and the omnipresent mass of Mount Olympus hulks to the west.

After 1.6 miles of up-and-down travel, the trail drops into a low saddle. A climber's trail continues along the ridgeline to the south, while the main path bends east to descend into the Grand Valley. The blue mirror of Grand Lake can be seen far below amid verdant forests on the valley floor. The alpine desert is particularly barren in this area; low-growing krummholz firs huddle in small clumps amid wide expanses of bare, rocky soil. These shrublike conifers are actually the same species as the spire-shaped firs that grow in more protected locales. When a young tree takes root on an exposed ridgetop like this one, the winter gales blow snow and particles of ice across the surface of the snowdrifts, abrading away any branches that rise above the snow line. Over time, this natural pruning creates a ground-hugging mat of branches that may represent a tree that is hundreds of years old.

Enjoy the beauty of the alpine scenery, pack a lunch for a sublime dining experience in the wilds, and search for rodents on the surrounding slopes and raptors in the skies. Be conscious of the fragility of this high alpine environment, and confine your activities to bare rock. After taking in the delights, retrace your steps to complete the hike.

The Elwha River

The valley of the Elwha River penetrates to the geographic center of the park, a deep, glacier-carved trough in the midst of crags. The Elwha band of S'Klallams once had a village along the Elwha's banks, since flooded by the waters of Lake Mills. Fierce hunters from this band ranged far up the valley in pursuit of elk. (The dam that created Lake Mills is slated for removal in 2009, freeing this wild and magnificent river from its concrete bonds.)

Later, members of the Press Expedition chose this corridor in their crossing of the range. This ragtag band of booze hounds and glory seekers required two months to trace the Elwha to its source and follow the North Fork of the Quinault down to civilization. (The same journey today, with the assistance of good trails, takes four or five days.) Along the way, the Press Expedition named many of the austere crags at the heart of the Olympics for the obscure newspaper barons who funded their expedition. In the late 1800s, homesteading activity occurred in the Geyser Valley part of the drainage, and several sturdy cabins remain to this day. Olympic Hot Springs, once a developed resort, has been returned to a natural state and offers an undeveloped alternative to Sol Duc Hot Springs, farther west.

Both Hurricane Ridge and Olympic Hot Springs Roads have fee entrance stations on them. There is a full-fledged visitor center in Port Angeles and a ranger station in the Elwha Valley. There is camping at the Elwha and Altaire Campgrounds in the Elwha Valley. Port Angeles offers all services required by the traveler, and there are limited supplies at the junction of U.S. Highway 101 and Olympic Hot Springs Road.

11 Madison Creek Falls

Type of hike: Out-and-back.
Total distance: 0.2 mile round-trip.
Elevation change: Minimal.

Approximate hiking time: 10 to 20 minutes.
Topo maps: USGS Elwha; Custom Correct *Hurricane Ridge*.

Finding the trailhead: Take U.S. Highway 101 west from Port Angeles, then follow Olympic Hot Springs Road south up the Elwha Valley. The Madison Creek Falls Trail begins from the parking area beside the entrance station.

The Hike

This paved pathway offers a gentle stroll on the floor of the Elwha River valley, visiting a stunning waterfall hidden at

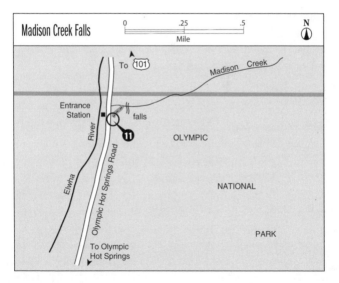

the edge of the valley. The trail is suited to all visitors and accommodates wheelchairs with ease. It begins near the Elwha River entrance station and wanders eastward across grassy meadows to reach an impressive waterfall on Madison Creek. Here the stream drops across a sheet cliff to reach the valley floor, and a lush mixture of hardwoods thrives in the abundant moisture of this pleasant pocket in the foothills. From the waterfall, turn around to return to the parking area.

12 Geyser Valley Loop

Type of hike: Loop.
Total distance: 5.6 miles.
Elevation change: 380-foot loss overall, 380-foot gain.

Approximate hiking time: 3 to 5 hours.
Topo maps: USGS Hurricane Hill, Custom Correct *Elwha Valley*.

Finding the trailhead: From U.S. Highway 101, follow Olympic Hot Springs Road up the Elwha Valley. Just beyond the ranger station, turn left onto Whiskey Bend Road. Follow this narrow, winding gravel road 4.4 miles to the trailhead at its end.

The Hike

This pleasant hike visits the bottomlands along the lower reaches of the Elwha River. The earliest white explorers to visit this area named it the Geyser Valley, fooled perhaps by swirling mists and the drumming of grouse into believing that there were thermal geysers in the area. At the turn of the twentieth century, a small number of homesteaders moved into the area, building rustic cabins with the abundant local timber and clearing small patches of forest to

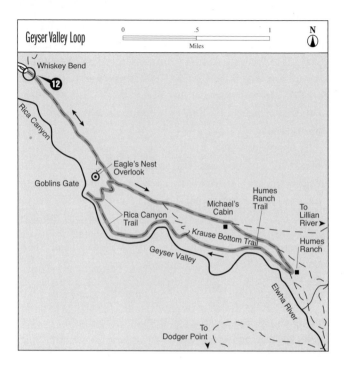

Geyser Valley Loop

0   .5   1
Miles

N

Whiskey Bend

12

Rica Canyon

Eagle's Nest
Overlook

Goblins Gate

Humes
Ranch
Trail

Michael's
Cabin

To
Lillian
River ▶

Rica Canyon
Trail

Krause Bottom Trail

Humes
Ranch

Geyser Valley

Elwha River

To
Dodger Point

plant their gardens. The homesteads have long been abandoned, but a few old cabins remain to delight the modern visitor. This loop trip also visits the Goblins Gate, a striking geological feature that marks the head of Rica Canyon.

From Whiskey Bend Trailhead, the trail runs southward along a forested hillside high above the valley floor. A spur path soon runs down to an overlook named the Eagle's Nest Overlook by the Press Expedition. This spot commands a fine view of the Elwha Valley, and the meadows of the former Anderson homestead can be seen across the river. Elk and black bear are sometimes seen in this bottomland clearing during the morning or evening. The trail then makes its way across the several burns of the 1977 Rica Canyon Fire. The fire site is recovering naturally with a dense growth of shrubs and saplings. The Rica Canyon Trail drops away in the middle of the first burn; follow the Elwha River Trail to the left. At the far edge of the burn is a junction with the Krause Bottom Trail.

Bear left to reach Michael's Cabin, one of the many Geyser Valley homesteads. This sturdy dwelling was once the property of a colorful resident known locally as "Cougar Mike," a nemesis of mountain lions noted for his sharp-shooting ability. The next meadow to the north is the former site of Geyser House, a ramshackle hostelry that was run by a former Seattle policeman known as "Doc" Ludden. This self-proclaimed "Bee Man of the Elwha" kept hives of honeybees and made his own honey.

The loop route now departs from the Elwha River Trail, descending toward the river bottoms on the Humes Ranch Trail. This trail descends obliquely through the trees, passing a junction with the Dodger Point Trail (bear right here). It then crosses diminutive Antelope Creek and descends sharply to reach the Humes Ranch after 0.4 mile. The cabin found here was built in 1900 by Grant and Will Humes, who were among the earliest homesteaders in the Elwha Valley. This dynamic pair of brothers ran an outfitting operation in the Olympic Mountains, running pack trains for expeditions of climbers, hunters, and sightseers.

A junction with the Geyser Valley Trail marked "Krause Bottom" lies at the lower edge of the clearing; bear right onto this trail to continue the loop hike. This trail descends to the lush river flats. Here clumps of gnarled vine maple are draped with mosses, and a mixed forest of red alder and

Douglas fir provides a rather sparse canopy. After 0.7 mile the Geyser Valley Trail rises to an elevated terrace to meet the Krause Bottom Trail.

The loop hike continues along the Geyser Valley Trail, but first take a brief stroll up the Krause Bottom Trail to visit the old Krause homestead. It occupies a meadowy bench sprinkled with ornamental fruit trees that have reverted to a more or less wild state. These trees are the remnants of the Krause orchard. It was planted by a German couple who homesteaded here in the mid-1890s, but a fire burned them out and they were forced to abandon their pioneering efforts. The clearing and orchard trees are the only trace that remains of their labors.

After visiting the Krause homestead site, hike west on the Geyser Valley Trail. It drops back into a quiet riverbottom forest, where the murmur of the river provides a soothing background for the twittering of birds. A luxuriant undergrowth of moss, vanilla leaf, and sword fern suffuses the forest with a soft green light. The trail emerges for the first time beside the Elwha River at an outcrop of unyielding stone that receives the full force of the water.

Just beyond this spot is the spur trail that follows the river downstream for 0.1 mile to an outcrop of bedrock that overlooks Goblins Gate. This interesting geological formation marks the entrance to Rica Canyon. It is an uplift of slate and sandstone that has been riven by the swirling turquoise waters of the Elwha over the course of centuries. The name reflects the imagination of early visitors who thought that they could discern the craggy faces of goblins amid the folds and crenellations of the rock walls.

To complete the loop, walk back to the Goblins Gate junction and follow the Rica Canyon Trail eastward across a forested terrace. It soon begins a stiff climb to meet the Elwha River Trail, zigzagging upward for 0.5 mile as it enters the Rica Canyon burn once more. Upon reaching the Elwha River Trail, turn left and retrace the initial leg of the hike to return to Whiskey Bend.

Key Points

0.0 Whiskey Bend Trailhead. Follow the Elwha River Trail southeast.

0.9 Spur path descends to Eagle's Nest Overlook. Visit the overlook and then continue southeast on Elwha River Trail.

1.2 Junction with Rica Canyon Trail. Stay left on Elwha River Trail.

1.6 Junction with Krause Bottom Trail. Stay left on Elwha River Trail.

1.9 Michael's Cabin and junction with Humes Ranch Trail. Turn right.

2.1 Junction with Dodger Point Trail. Bear right.

2.3 Humes Ranch. Turn right onto Geyser Valley Trail, following signs for Krause Bottom.

3.0 Junction with Krause Bottom Trail. Visit Krause homestead site, then hike west toward Rica Canyon Trail.

3.9 Junction with Goblins Gate Spur Trail. Hike to overlook (0.2-mile round-trip), then ascend on Rica Canyon Trail.

4.4 Junction with Elwha River Trail. Turn left to finish the hike.

5.6 Hike ends at Whiskey Bend Trailhead.

13 Olympic Hot Springs

Type of hike: Out-and-back.
Total distance: 4.9 miles round-trip.
Elevation change: 190-foot gain, 60-foot loss to springs.

Approximate hiking time: 2.5 to 4 hours (add more time if you want to take a dip).
Topo maps: USGS Mount Carrie; Custom Correct *Lake Crescent–Happy Lake Ridge.*

Finding the trailhead: From U.S. Highway 101 west of Port Angeles, follow Olympic Hot Springs Road, which ascends the Elwha Valley into the park. Stay on the main road as you pass the Elwha Ranger Station; go past the Altaire Campground to the end of the road.

The Hike

This old roadbed follows Boulder Creek up to the undeveloped hot springs on its south bank. The hot springs are quite popular with local weekenders; visit them during the week to avoid the crowds. These hot pools are not tested for the presence of pathogens; bathe at your own risk.

For the first 2.2 miles, the trek follows an old paved road along the forested banks of Boulder Creek. A second-growth forest of Douglas fir shades the old road, and slide alders are beginning to encroach along its edges. This road ends at a junction below the Boulder Creek Campground. The path to Olympic Hot Springs continues upstream along the creek, then crosses it and turns back to the east to reach the hot pools. There was once a developed resort here, but it has long since been torn down. The pools have been returned to a natural state and are scattered across the hillside above the stream. Each pool has its own temperature, and the lowest

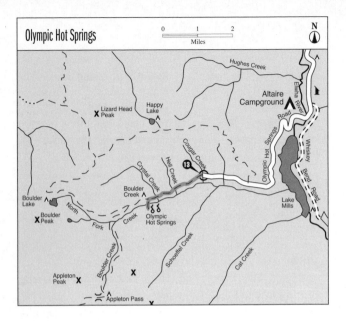

pools have mud bottoms while the upper pools are lined with rock. After visiting the pools, retrace the trail back to the trailhead.

Key Points

- **0.0** Boulder Creek Trailhead.
- **2.2** Junction with Olympic Hot Springs Spur Trail. Bear left.
- **2.3** Trail crosses bridge over Boulder Creek to access first of the hot pools.
- **2.4** Uppermost hot pool.
- **4.9** Return to the trailhead.

Lake Crescent and the Sol Duc River

This northern fringe of the Olympic Mountains is dominated by heavily forested peaks. The low basins were originally carved by glaciers and now bear the drainages of the Lyre and Sol Duc Rivers. Sol Duc means "sparkling waters" in the dialect of the S'Klallams, and this great stream is born in an area of tremendous geothermal activity. Waters heated by molten magma rise through faults in the Juan de Fuca Plate, leaking to the surface at Sol Duc Hot Springs. These waters have been harnessed in swimming pool form at a full-scale resort within the park.

Lake Crescent is one of the primary attractions of the area. This large body of water is clear and cold, surrounded by imposing peaks. This lake attained its current size when a landslide blocked its eastern outlet, and the water level rose until it poured over the northern lip of the basin to form the Lyre River. This new outlet stream was too turbulent to admit the passage of sea-run rainbow and cutthroat trout that inhabited the lake, and these isolated stocks evolved into the Beardslee and Crescenti trout, respectively.

There are ranger stations near Sol Duc Hot Springs and on Barnes Point on the south shore of Lake Crescent. The Sol Duc Hot Springs Resort, Lake Crescent Lodge, and Log Cabin Resort provide lodgings within the national park, and there are campgrounds near the hot springs and at the western end of Lake Crescent. An entrance fee is charged on Sol Duc Hot Springs Road. The Fairholm general store at the western end of Lake Crescent and the Sol Duc Hot Springs camp store are the only nearby source of supplies.

14 Marymere Falls

Type of hike: Out-and-back.
Total distance: 1.8 miles round-trip.
Elevation change: 80-foot gain.

Approximate hiking time: 1 to 1.5 hours.
Topo maps: USGS Lake Crescent; Custom Correct *Lake Crescent–Happy Lake Ridge*.

Finding the trailhead: Take U.S. Highway 101 to mile 228 on the south shore of Lake Crescent, then take a short side road north to the Storm King Ranger Station. The trail begins from this point and crosses underneath the highway.

The Hike

From the shores of Lake Crescent, this trail offers a short trip into a beautiful old-growth forest of Douglas fir, then crosses Barnes Creek and climbs a steep stairway to Marymere Falls, a 90-foot cascade. There are interpretive signs along the way, and the forest portion of the trail can be readily negotiated by wheelchairs.

To begin the hike, follow the paved pathway that runs south from the ranger station. It soon ducks through an underpass beneath the highway, emerging among the tall columns of a Douglas fir forest. This is a true old-growth stand, and new seedlings can take root only as the most ancient trees die of old age and fall to the forest floor, creating sunny openings in the canopy. The vigor of this stand of trees is due in part to the richness of the alluvial soil, brought down by Barnes Creek and deposited in a delta as the creek waters entered Lake Crescent and slowed to allow their load of silt to settle out.

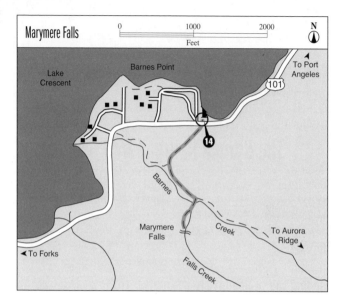

Upon reaching the upper edge of the delta, there is a junction with the trail that leads up Barnes Creek to Aurora Ridge. Turn right as the Marymere Falls Trail leads to a log footbridge over Barnes Creek. There is a loose woodland of red cedar on the far bank, and here the trail becomes a steep but well-built stairway that leads up to the base of Marymere Falls. The falls is a slender ribbon of water brought down from Aurora Ridge by a tributary stream, and its constant mist supports a growth of ferns and mosses on the surrounding rock. From the viewing platform, turn around to complete the hike.

Key Points

0.0 Storm King Ranger Station.

0.4 Trail is joined by cutoff trail from Lake Crescent Lodge.

0.5 Storm King Trail departs to left. Stay right, on main trail.

0.7 Marymere Falls Trail splits away from Barnes Creek Trail. Turn right and cross log footbridge over Barnes Creek.

0.9 Trail reaches viewing platform at base of Marymere Falls.

1.8 Return to the ranger station.

15 The Spruce Railroad Trail

Type of hike: Shuttle.
Total distance: 4 miles one way.
Elevation change: 260-foot gain, 260-foot loss.

Approximate hiking time: 2 to 3.5 hours.
Topo maps: USGS Lake Crescent; Custom Correct *Lake Crescent–Happy Lake Ridge.*

Finding the trailhead: Take U.S. Highway 101 to a junction with East Beach Road, at mile 232 just east of Lake Crescent. Follow this winding, paved road 3.2 miles, passing the Log Cabin Resort and turning left onto another paved road bearing a sign for the Spruce Railroad Trail. This road crosses the Lyre River to reach a parking area near some private residences. The trail begins from a sign on the west side of the road. The trail ends at the end of Camp David Jr. Road, which departs from US 101 just west of the Fairholm general store at the western end of Lake Crescent.

The Hike

This trail offers a gentle stroll along the north shore of Lake Crescent, making a point-to-point hike that is described here from east to west. It follows an old railbed that was built during World War I to transport Sitka spruce from the then-inaccessible western part of the peninsula to the aircraft fac-

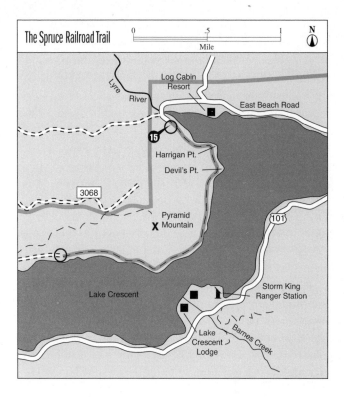

tories. Sitka spruce has a superior ratio of strength to weight, and was therefore coveted for the making of biplane airframes. The railroad was completed in a remarkable time of only six weeks, but the war was over before the first logs rolled eastward on the rails. The railway was active through the 1950s, when it was abandoned and subsequently turned into a trail. It is one of the only trails in Olympic National Park where mountain bikes are permitted. For hikers who lack the time or inclination to hike the entire trail, Devil's

Point makes an ideal turnaround point. Watch out for poison oak if you get off the trail.

The trail begins by running inland from North Shore Road, climbing gently to reach the old railroad grade. As the railbed runs southward, it passes through a mixed forest of red alder and Douglas fir, skirting inland to avoid private residences along the lakeshore. It then descends to the shoreline, although dense trees screen out views of the water. A rough spur path to Harrigan Point brings the traveler to a grassy spit that offers the first unobstructed vistas of the hike.

A short distance farther, the main trail climbs a bit to round the rocky headland of Devil's Point. A tunnel was blasted through the bedrock of the point to accommodate the railway, but it has since been sealed off with rocky debris. The point itself offers fine views of the north arm of the lake and Mount Storm King rising above the waters to the south. Pacific madrone thrives in the thin soils of this sunny locale. A bridge soon arches above the waters of a narrow and rocky cove. The imposing rock faces that rise all around this inlet are the exposed foundation of Pyramid Mountain.

Just beyond the bridge are fine views of the western arm of the lake, with the towering green wall of Aurora Ridge dominating its south shore. The next stretch of shoreline is frequently punctuated by openings where the trail skirts the base of sheer cliffs. Lake Crescent Lodge occupies the alluvial delta of Barnes Creek on the far side of the lake. Soon the trail reaches a second tunnel, and the eastern entrance of this one has not been blocked. The tunnel is choked with rubble and rotting timber, however, and exploring it would be an unsafe proposition. Beside the trail, sections of old rail are reminiscent of earlier times as the path makes its way through sun-dappled groves of red alder to reach the western trailhead. Just before arriving at the trailhead outhouse, the path departs from the railbed and drops to meet the end of Camp David Jr. Road.

Key Points

- **0.0** East trailhead.
- **0.8** Harrigan Point.
- **1.1** Devil's Point.
- **2.9** Second tunnel.
- **4.0** West trailhead and your vehicle or a ride.

16 Sol Duc Falls

Type of hike: Out-and-back.
Total distance: 1.5 miles round-trip.
Elevation change: Minimal.

Approximate hiking time: 45 minutes to 1.5 hours.
Topo maps: USGS Bogachiel Peak; Custom Correct *Seven Lakes Basin-Hoh.*

Finding the trailhead: From U.S. Highway 101, drive about 13 miles on Sol Duc Hot Springs Road to a large parking lot at its end. The trail departs from the south end of this lot.

The Hike

From the trailhead, a broad path winds eastward through the towering bottomland forest. The trail forks at the Sol Duc Falls shelter. Follow the right fork down to the river, where a stout bridge and viewing area allow close inspection of this

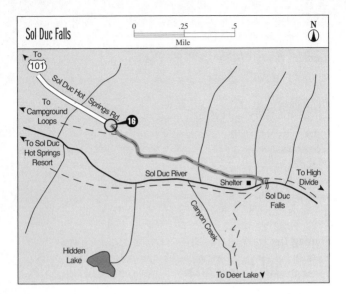

Sol Duc Falls

unusual cataract. As the river wore a channel through the stone of the valley floor, it encountered a hard, resistant stratum of stone that was tilted vertically and cut diagonally across the river channel. Immediately south of this hard layer was a layer of weak, easily eroded rock through which the waters soon wore a deep path. The result is Sol Duc Falls, where the river spills in an angled curtain across the sill of resistant rock and lands 20 feet below in a deep cleft. From the bridge, retrace the path to return to the trailhead.

Key Points

0.0 Trailhead.

0.1 Junction with spur from Sol Duc Campground. Continue straight ahead.

0.7 Loop trail splits at Sol Duc Falls shelter. Turn right.

0.8 Bridge spans Sol Duc River at Sol Duc Falls.

1.5 Retrace your steps to the trailhead.

17 Lover's Lane

Type of hike: Loop.
Total distance: 6 miles.
Elevation change: Minimal.
Approximate hiking time: 2.5 to 4.5 hours.

Topo maps: USGS Bogachiel Peak; Custom Correct *Seven Lakes Basin–Hoh.*

Finding the trailhead: From U.S. Highway 101, drive about 12 miles on Sol Duc Hot Springs Road to the Sol Duc Hot Springs Resort. The trek begins and ends at a marked trailhead beside the resort at the western edge of the parking lot.

The Hike

This trail links Sol Duc Hot Springs with Sol Duc Falls, offering an easy loop of 6 miles through pristine old growth and the Sol Duc auto campground. The forest here mixes the elements of the rain forests to the west with plants of the rain shadow country to the east.

The trail begins by passing behind the swimming pools of Sol Duc Hot Springs. Early in the trek, ranks of moss-draped vine maple arch over the path, while nurse logs and old stumps provide aerial platforms for mosses and seedlings. Near the falls, the more open woodland is dominated by Douglas fir, and broad glades between the trees are populated by bracken, lady, and sword ferns. After 3 miles, the trail

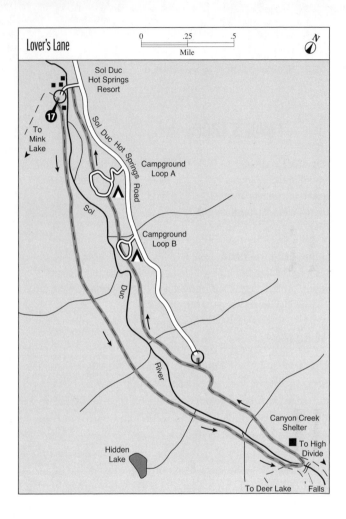

Lover's Lane

0   .25   .5
Mile

N

Sol Duc Hot Springs Resort

To Mink Lake

17

Sol Duc Hot Springs Road

Campground Loop A

Campground Loop B

Sol

Duc

River

Hidden Lake

Canyon Creek Shelter

To High Divide

To Deer Lake   Falls

reaches spectacular Sol Duc Falls; from this point, the route follows the Sol Duc Falls Trail downstream toward the trailhead, then follows signs to the campground. It wanders close to the east bank of the river for more deep forest scenery, crossing through two campground loops (follow the signs) to return to the lodge.

Key Points

0.0 Lover's Lane Trailhead.

0.1 Junction with trail to Mink Lake. Bear left on wider path.

2.9 Junction with trail to Deer Lake and the High Divide. Turn left.

3.0 Bridge over Sol Duc River at Sol Duc Falls.

3.1 Shelter and junction with trail that follows Sol Duc River. Bear left.

3.7 Junction with trail to Sol Duc Campground loops. Turn left onto it.

5.1 Trail leaves Campground Loop B at site 62.

5.3 Trail leaves Campground Loop A at site 21.

5.5 Trail passes amphitheater.

5.8 Trail emerges onto road. Turn left and follow road to Sol Duc Hot Springs.

6.0 Hike ends at Lover's Lane Trailhead.

The Western
Rain Forests

The westward-flowing rivers of the Olympic Peninsula flow from massive glaciers at the crest of the range and churn through braided channels to reach the Pacific Ocean. Deep, U-shaped valleys receive more than 150 inches of rain each year, giving rise to the ancient temperate rain forests for which the region is famous. Here trees may be more than 1,000 years old, and every surface—living and dead—is covered with smaller forms of plant life. A few of the western trails penetrate all the way up into alpine regions, offering views of active glaciers that receive up to 20 feet of snow each winter.

The Hoh and Quinault valleys have the best access and receive the greatest attention from tourists. The Hoh Rainforest has a major visitor center and campground and a fee station at the park entrance. There are also several free campgrounds outside the park entrance. Lake Quinault is another focal point for visitors, with several resorts along its southern shore. There is a campground and a seasonal ranger station at Graves Creek and on the North Fork of the Quinault River, and the district ranger station is on Lake Quinault North Shore Road. The Forest Service has a visitor center and several campgrounds on the south shore of the lake.

The other river valleys are wilder and more remote, offering a more primitive wilderness experience. There is a National Park Service campground at the end of Queets

River Road, while various state agencies administer camp-grounds on the South Fork of the Hoh and Bogachiel Rivers. Supplies can be procured at Amanda Park, Quinault, or in Forks, and there are also a few stores along Hoh Rain-forest Road.

18 Spruce Nature Trail

Type of hike: Loop.
Total distance: 1.3 miles.
Elevation change: Minimal.
Approximate hiking time: 45
minutes to 1.5 hours.

Topo maps: USGS Mount Tom;
Custom Correct *Seven Lakes
Basin-Hoh.*

Finding the trailhead: From Forks, drive south on U.S. Highway
101 to mile 178.5. Turn east onto paved Hoh River Road. Drive 18
miles to the trailhead and visitor center at road's end.

The Hike

One of the two popular interpretive walks in the Hoh Rainforest, this trail visits impressive stands of old-growth Sitka
spruce that grow along the Hoh River. Interpretive plaques
along the way explain the ecology of the rain forest. The trail
is paved and accessible to wheelchairs.

This level trek begins from the midpoint of the short visitor center loop path, and soon makes its way to an old river
terrace from which the stout boles of spruce and Douglas fir
tower skyward. This is old-growth rain forest at its finest: The
ancient conifers are widely spaced, and plenty of sunlight
streams through to support the multiple canopy layers of
younger trees, tall shrubs, and a rich ground cover of ferns,
mosses, and woodland flowers.

As the path approaches the river, it visits old flood channels that are shaded by groves of red alder. This tree is a spe-
cialist at colonizing flood-scoured openings, where thin soils
and ample sunlight favor alder seedlings over other plants. At
the river's edge, the trail turns downstream to follow the

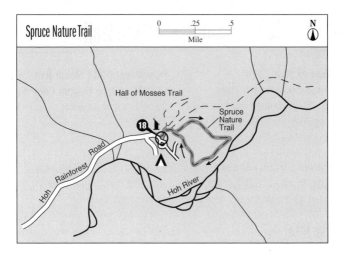

0   .25   .5
Mile

N

Hall of Mosses Trail

18

Spruce
Nature
Trail

Hoh Rainforest Road

Hoh River

braided channels that course across a barren plain of gravel. Geologically this is a young river, and its swift current pushes a heavy load of gravel down the riverbed, clogging its own channel and forcing the water to seek a new and lower pathway to the sea. After a brief riverside journey, the trail turns inland through a tangle of vine maples draped with spikemoss. The path soon strikes a spring-fed creek and follows it back to the visitor center.

19 Hall Of Mosses Nature Trail

Type of hike: Loop.
Total distance: 0.8 mile.
Elevation change: 60-foot gain.
Approximate hiking time: 30 to
60 minutes.

Topo maps: USGS Mount Tom,
Mount Olympus; Custom Correct
Seven Lakes Basin-Hoh.

Finding the trailhead: From Forks, drive south on U.S. Highway
101 to mile 178.5. Turn east onto paved Hoh River Road. Drive 18
miles to the trailhead and visitor center at road's end.

The Hike

This trail forms a loop through the celebrated Hoh Rainforest, visiting a stand of ghostly old bigleaf maples draped
with spikemoss. There are signs along the way to enlighten
the visitor about the plants of the old-growth forest.

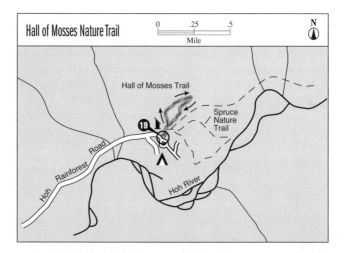

From its beginning on the visitor center loop, the Hall of Mosses Trail climbs briskly to the top of a spruce-clad terrace. Bear left as the trail splits and then makes its way among the trunks of enormous conifers. Nearing the midpoint of the loop, the trail enters groves of bigleaf maple, long streamers of spikemoss hanging from their massive branches. When soaked with rain, the weight of the moss becomes so great that even a stout branch may break off under the strain. Aerial plants like spikemoss, known to ecologists as epiphytes, are one of the hallmarks of a true rain forest. Another epiphyte common to this area is the licorice fern, which grows from moss beds on tree trunks and fallen logs. Watch for nurse logs, fallen trees that have become seedbeds for shrubs and seedlings, as the trail makes its way back to the visitor center.

20 Hoh River

Type of hike: Out-and-back.
Total distance: Up to 10 miles round-trip, depending on turn-around point.
Elevation change: Minimal.

Approximate hiking time: Up to 8 hours.
Topo maps: USGS Mount Tom; Custom Correct *Seven Lakes Basin–Hoh*.

Finding the trailhead: From Forks, drive south on U.S. Highway 101 to mile 178.5. Turn east onto paved Hoh River Road. Drive 18 miles to the trailhead and visitor center at road's end.

The Hike

The journey starts on the paved walkway that is shared with the Spruce Nature Trail system. The Hoh River Trail soon

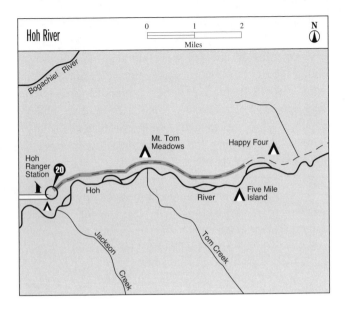

splits off to the northeast—a wide, smooth path that runs across the forest duff. The lower portion of the Hoh valley is robed in a magnificent rain forest, where the enormous boles of the Sitka spruce rise like pillars from the verdant forest floor. Mosses, ferns, and conifer seedlings carpet every level spot, including fallen logs and standing stumps. The trail wanders close to the river at times, affording campsites for short-range travelers. It soon crosses a substantial stream, and soon afterward a smaller cousin. At this point, Mount Tom can be glimpsed to the southeast through a curtain of foliage.

Soon afterward, a spur path leads to Tom Creek Meadows, a camping area situated in a grassy grove of red alder on the riverbank. The Hoh River meanders across a broad bed of outwash gravel, shifting its course after every major storm. Beyond this point, a handful of western red cedars are conspicuously present in the overstory; some attain magnificent proportions. At mile 4.5 the trail crosses a well-drained terrace. Here ancient spruces rise rank on rank with little intervening vegetation to mask the magnificent vertical landscape.

The route then drops to the river bottoms, crossing dry sloughs and tarrying among tall alders and squat, moss-draped vine maples. The Five Mile Island campsites are along the bottomland at mile 5. This is probably the farthest point a day traveler could comfortably reach. Turn around here to complete the hike.

Key Points

- **0.0** Hoh Rainforest Visitor Center.
- **0.2** Hoh River Trail departs from Spruce Nature Trail system.
- **2.5** Twin Creek Falls.
- **2.9** Spur trail to Tom Creek Meadows.
- **5.0** Five Mile Island campsites mark turnaround point.
- **10.0** Return to the visitor center.

21 The South Fork of the Hoh River

Type of hike: Out-and-back.
Total distance: 8 miles round-trip.
Elevation change: 110-foot gain, 140-foot loss.

Approximate hiking time: 4 to 7 hours.
Topo maps: USGS Mount Tom; Custom Correct *Mount Olympus Climber's Map*.

Finding the trailhead: From mile 176 on U.S. Highway 101 (just south of the Hoh Oxbow Campground), turn southeast onto paved Clearwater Road. Drive 8 miles and turn left at signs for the South Fork Hoh Campground. Follow markers for Road 1000 (avoid other marked turnoffs) for 10 miles, past the South Fork Hoh Campground, to the trailhead at road's end.

The Hike

This remote trail offers a quiet stroll through the rain forest and big timber along the South Fork of the Hoh River. The bottomlands of the South Fork are typified by grassy meadows and thickets of hardwoods. A few ancient conifers rise over all. Due to its remoteness, the South Fork of the Hoh receives relatively few visitors and thus is a good rain forest destination for solitude seekers.

From the trailhead, the path descends through a stand of young spruce, passing a hairpin turn on a closed logging road before veering away to the east. The forest is less dense beyond the park boundary, with a complex overstory featuring a variety of canopy heights. Huge Sitka spruce and western hemlock tower above all, while their younger relatives vie for openings in the canopy. Vine maple is a common understory shrub here, and a variety of forbs and ferns decorate the forest floor.

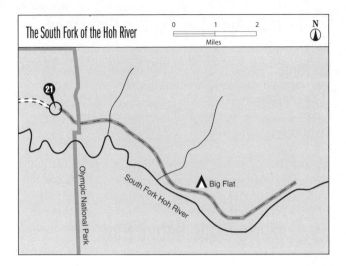

The descent continues past a fair-size stream before dropping the traveler onto Big Flat, a broad swath of bottomland on the north bank of the South Fork. Potential campsites abound as the trail continues eastward just out of sight of the river. Ancient spruce trees are spaced hundreds of feet apart, with an understory sometimes crowded with red alder and vine maple and at other times almost entirely absent. The path swings next to an overlook of the river, then crosses through a dense growth of salmonberry on its way inland again. Higher, well-drained benches support stands of Sitka spruce that commonly exceed 10 feet in diameter.

As the path nears the river once again, grassy savannahs separate the conifers and render the trail difficult to detect. It can be followed, however, beyond the next river overlook that features views of Hoh Peak. After crossing a considerable amount of deadfall, the trail peters out on the eastern end of the flats. A hillside descends steeply to meet the river here, blocking further progress to the east. Turn around here to complete the hike.

Key Points

0.0   Trailhead.

0.5   Olympic National Park boundary and registration station.

1.5   Trail enters Big Flat.

4.0   End of trail.

8.0   Turn around and return to the trailhead.

22 Maple Glade Nature Trail

Type of hike: Loop.
Total distance: 0.5 mile.
Elevation change: Minimal.
Approximate hiking time: 20 to 45 minutes.

Topo maps: USGS Finley Creek (trail not shown); Custom Correct *Quinault-Colonel Bob.*

Finding the trailhead: From Amanda Park, drive north on U.S. Highway 101 to Lake Quinault North Shore Road. Follow this paved road for 6 miles to reach the Lake Quinault Ranger Station (NPS). The hike begins opposite the ranger station.

The Hike

This self-guided trail begins next to the Lake Quinault Ranger Station and loops through the lush rain forest bottomlands beside Kestner Creek. A self-guiding pamphlet is available at the beginning of the trail and offers further insights into rain forest ecology.

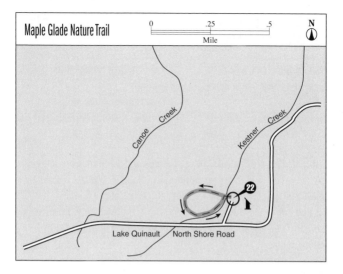

0   .25   .5

Mile

N

The trail begins by crossing Kestner Creek. Coarse gravels have been deposited here during floods, creating a well-drained soil that favors the bigleaf maple. Enormous specimens of this rain forest hardwood grow here, their gnarled branches draped with long streamers of spikemoss. Watch for the ubiquitous banana slug, which thrives here on an abundance of hardwood leaf litter.

The maples are interspersed with a few graceful old hemlocks and Sitka spruces, while dense groves of red alder occupy areas of disturbance by fire or flooding. These bottoms serve as winter range for Roosevelt elk, which mold the forest ecosystem by browsing away young trees and shrubs to create a more open understory. The result of their foraging efforts is a parklike woodland underlain by ground-hugging oxalis, violets, and buttercups.

23 Irely Lake

Type of hike: Out-and-back.
Total distance: 2.6 miles round-trip.
Elevation change: Minimal.

Approximate hiking time: 1.5 to 3 hours.
Topo maps: USGS Mount Christie; Custom Correct *Quinault-Colonel Bob.*

Finding the trailhead: Take U.S. Highway 101 north from Amanda Park to reach Lake Quinault North Shore Road. Follow this road eastward; it is paved for the first 7 miles. Bear left at the junction at mile 12 and continue up North Shore Road for the remaining 2.6 miles to the Irely Lake Trailhead, which is across the road from the North Fork Campground.

The Hike

The trail begins in the rain forest river bottoms of the Quinault's North Fork. It runs northward among the stout trunks of old-growth red cedar and Sitka spruce, climbing in short bursts across the forested benchlands. Ferns and mosses grow from every available surface, suffusing the landscape with green. After 0.7 mile the trail crosses tiny Irely Creek and begins to follow its meandering, brush-choked channel. Salmonberries and thimbleberries grow side by side along the stream's course.

Soon a spur trail splits away to the left, running through a profusion of red huckleberries en route to the benches overlooking Irely Lake. (The berries ripen in August.) This large rain forest pool is surrounded by wet meadows, forming a rare and important pocket of wetland in the midst of the conifers. During the winter rainy season, the lake fills to the brim with water, but during the summer the water level

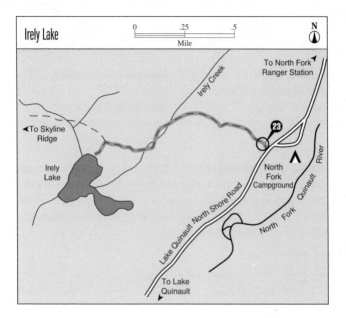

drops as the lake water drains away through underground channels. Ospreys, waterfowl, and beavers are commonly seen at the lake and the surrounding marshes. During winter, herds of Roosevelt elk are sometimes spotted here. There is a primitive camping area at the north end, but mosquitoes are known to be fierce here. Retrace the trail from the lake to return to the trailhead.

Key Points

- **0.0** Irely Lake Trailhead.
- **0.7** Trail crosses Irely Creek.
- **1.1** Spur path to Irely Lake.
- **1.3** Irely Lake.
- **2.6** Return to the trailhead.

24 Cascading Terraces Nature Trail

Type of hike: Loop.
Total distance: 1 mile.
Elevation change: 40 foot loss and gain.

Approximate hiking time: 30 to 60 minutes.
Topo maps: USGS Mount Hoquiam; Custom Correct *Quinault-Colonel Bob.*

Finding the trailhead: From U.S. Highway 101 at mile 125.5 (just south of Amanda Park), turn east onto Lake Quinault South Shore Road. The pavement ends after 7.8 miles, and after another 11 miles the road reaches the Graves Creek Campground. The trail begins at the end of the campground loop.

The Hike

This self-guiding nature trail begins at the far end of the Graves Creek Campground loop. More interesting for its diversity of forest types than for ancient trees, this 1-mile loop traverses old river terraces and abandoned channels as it wanders the alluvial floodplain of the Quinault River. Here the loop is described in a counterclockwise direction.

The path begins by running down the valley; bear right at the first intersection to begin the loop hike. It visits groves of climax Sitka spruce where seedlings take root on mossy nurse logs. It then wanders through galleries of gnarled bigleaf maples draped with clubmoss, punctuated by tall columns of black cottonwood. These hardwood groves mark the early colonization efforts as the forest overtakes the former riverbed. The path crosses grassy clearings and approaches the riverbank from time to time, allowing visitors an insight into the earliest beginning of colonizers like

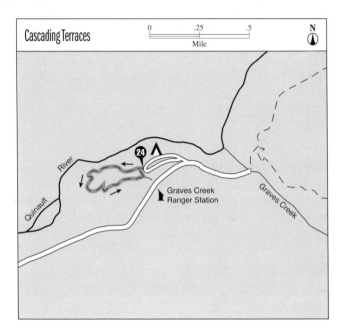

Cascading Terraces

0   .25   .5
Mile

N

Quinault River

24

Graves Creek
Ranger Station

Graves Creek

the red alder and Douglas fir. As the path wanders inland on
the return leg, see if you can identify the elevated river bars
and former channels, and note which types of trees and
undergrowth thrive in each.

The Olympic Coastline

The wild and rugged Olympic coast is the site of ceaseless change. Wave action weathers arches and sea stacks from resistant blocks of sandstone, then slowly abrades them down to nothing. The fractured rock of the coves is constantly slumping onto the beach, then is carried away by the waves. Flood-gorged rivers discharge great plumes of silt and debris into the ocean, forming long spits at their mouths. Enormous logs are washed out to sea by these rivers; the logs are stripped and polished by the surf and then cast up on the beach. The incessant pounding of the waves, as well as the periodic tempests of wintertime, are constantly at work tearing down the coastline and building it anew.

This environment of endless upheaval is also the site of one of the most diverse biological communities in the Pacific Northwest. Tide pools harbor an almost infinite array of invertebrate life amid a lush growth of aquatic plants. Gulls, mergansers, ospreys, and bald eagles wheel on the ocean breezes, while oystercatchers and sandpipers patrol the beaches and rocks. The offshore islands teem with marine mammals, featuring sea otters, gray whales, orcas, harbor seals, and the endangered Steller's sea lion. Such a bounty of marine life formed the economic backbone of the coastal Indian villages, which have stood here from time immemorial.

Most of the coastline can be hiked, but a tide table is a must because heavy surf renders most of the headlands impassable at high tide. Tide tables are posted at most trailheads, and free copies are usually offered as well. Avoid hiking around headlands on an incoming tide, and use common sense at all times. Changing weather patterns can result in higher tides than expected, especially when a storm is brewing. In addition, the surf often tosses huge (and deadly) logs around like matchsticks, and in many cases these surf logs are waterlogged and invisible beneath the waves. Do not swim in the surf of unprotected beaches; venture into the water only in protected areas that have little wave action. NOTE: The water is extremely cold, even in summer.

Developed areas near the coast can be found at Lake Ozette, Mora, and Kalaloch. Kalaloch (pronounced "kuh-LAY-lock") has its own lodge, and campgrounds and ranger stations can be found at all of these locations. Lake Ozette is a popular (though remote) destination, and its small campground is often full. A private store called the Lost Resort has some supplies and extra campsites. Clallam Bay, Forks, and, to a lesser extent, Kalaloch offer groceries and other supplies.

25 Cape Flattery

Type of hike: Out-and-back.
Total distance: 1.2 miles round-trip.
Elevation loss: 200 feet.

Approximate hiking time: 1 hour.
Topo maps: Cape Flattery; Custom Correct *North Olympic Coast.*

Finding the trailhead: From the west end of the town of Neah Bay, take Cape Flattery Road. After 2.5 miles, stay right at the intersection and follow the signs for Cape Flattery as the road turns from pavement to gravel and ends at the trailhead. A visitors' permit from the Makah Indian Reservation is required. The permit can be purchased in Neah Bay.

The Hike

This hike makes a short traverse through the Makah tribal wilderness to reach the crest of Cape Flattery, where stark cliffs rise above sea stacks and grottoes carved out by the thundering surf. This spot is one of the most dramatic "land's ends" on Earth, marking the northwesternmost point in the coterminous United States. Cape Flattery was named by Captain James Cook, the European discoverer of the Hawaiian Islands, who named this important nautical landmark that "flattered" him with the hopes of finding a safe harbor (there was none). Of course, the Makah people and other Native Americans had been using this area for many thousands of years to hunt, fish, and gather seagull eggs.

The hike begins on a wide path that descends steadily through heavy forest. Most of the big trees are red cedars and western hemlocks, with red alders present in abundance as well. The path soon levels off to become a boardwalk

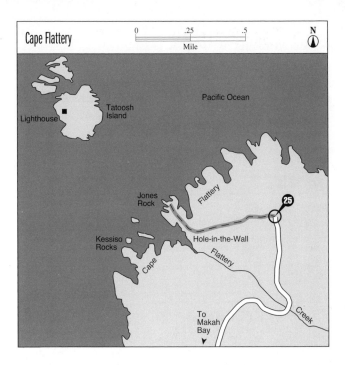

crossing a small swamp on an elevated bench, then becomes
a steady (and sometimes slippery) drop through the hemlocks. Watch for giant specimens of Sitka spruce as the path
makes its way onto a narrow, wooded promontory high
above the surf. Soon the first observation platform can be
seen to the south, offering views of sea stacks and the Hole-
in-the-Wall, a deep, fjordlike cove guarded by sheer cliffs.
There are two more observation decks on the north side of
the promontory en route to land's end, and these high
perches overlook deep caves and grottoes whittled into the
sandstone of the Cape by the booming surf.

The path ends at a platform atop that farthest-reaching pillar of stone on Cape Flattery. From here, panoramic views take in the striking architecture of coves and pillars both north and south, as well as the turtle-shell back of Tatoosh Island with its squat lighthouse. This islet, named for the fierce leader Tatooche of the Makah people, provides a rookery for sea lions and sea birds, which are often spotted hunting in the surrounding waters.

Key Points

0.0 Trailhead.

0.3 First observation platform above Hole-in-the-Wall.

0.6 Trail ends at tip of Cape Flattery.

1.2 Return to the trailhead.

26 Shi Shi Beach

Type of hike: Out-and-back.
Total distance: 4.4 miles round-trip.
Elevation change: 195-foot gain, 235-foot loss.

Approximate hiking time: 2 to 4 hours.
Topo maps: USGS Makah Bay, Ozette (for Point of the Arches); Custom Correct *North Olympic Coast.*

Finding the trailhead: From the west end of the town of Neah Bay, take Cape Flattery Road. After 2.5 miles, turn left onto Hobuck Road, staying left and following signs for the Makah National Fish Hatchery. The road approaches the coastline at Hobuck Beach, swings inland to cross the Sooes River, then swings close to the coast again at Tsoo Yess Beach. At the far end of the beach, the road climbs a wooded bluff to reach the well-marked Shi Shi Trailhead at

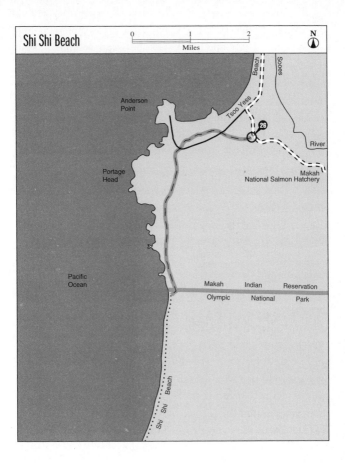

Shi Shi Beach

0   1   2
Miles

N

Anderson
Point

Tsoo Yess

Beach

Sooes

26

River

Portage
Head

Makah
National Salmon Hatchery

Pacific
Ocean

Makah   Indian   Reservation

Olympic   National   Park

Shi Shi Beach

mile 4.5. A tribal permit is necessary to hike on these lands. It can be purchased in Neah Bay.

The Hike

This new trail was recently rebuilt to offer access for day hikers to Shi Shi Beach, one of the more striking areas on the Olympic coastline. The good news is that access to this beach is now fast and easy; the bad news is that Shi Shi Beach, once a secluded destination for backcountry beach hikers, has turned into a somewhat busy day-hike destination, spoiling the remoteness once found here. As mentioned, all visitors on this trail will need a visitors' pass from the Makah Tribe to cross the tribal lands along the way, and overnight campers will also need a backcountry permit from Olympic National Park (the nearest ranger stations are far away at Ozette and Forks). Visitors should leave their pets at home, as they are not allowed past the Olympic National Park boundary or along Shi Shi Beach itself. For a long day hike, travelers can walk the beach southward for an additional 3 miles to reach Point of the Arches.

The trek begins on a mix of boardwalk and footpath that winds through several logged-over areas, by turns a dense growth of young hemlocks and a clearing crowded with a riot of underbrush. After crossing a well-worn track (the former Shi Shi trail, which crosses private property), the path tunnels through heavy vegetation to reach a cantilever bridge that spans a boggy rivulet choked with skunk cabbage. Here the path visits a wonderful grove of ancient spruce, hemlock, and cedar. Watch for the telltale buttress roots at the base of the big trees, indicating that they got their start atop elevated stumps or nurse logs as young seedlings.

The path now climbs several small hills as it rises through the forest to intersect the original trail, arrowing through the forest. The hike adopts this original trail for a gradual climb through a stand of red alder. A narrow defile between two steep hillsides marks the high point of the hike. As the trail drops gradually through the trees, a series of muddy spots must be negotiated. Soon the path is wandering through groves of stately hemlocks, punctuated here and there by scruffy Alaska yellow cedars and massive specimens of Sitka spruce. The pounding of the surf is now audible below, but it is not until the trail reaches the top of the grade down to Shi Shi Beach that you will get an unobstructed view of the water.

At the boundary of Olympic National Park, a veritable staircase of tree roots plummets down the forested face of the bluffs to deposit the traveler at the north end of Shi Shi Beach. A small cluster of arches and pinnacles graces the surf near at hand, while the jagged teeth of Point of the Arches rise to the south, a 3-mile beach walk away.

Key Points

0.0   Trailhead is two driveways before the hatchery.

0.6   Cantilever bridge.

1.1   Trail crosses through narrow saddle.

2.1   Olympic National Park boundary. Trail begins a steep descent.

2.2   Shi Shi Beach.

4.4   Return to the trailhead.

27 **Cape Alava**

Type of hike: Out-and-back.
Total distance: 6.6 miles round-trip to Cape Alava; 8.6 miles round-trip to the Wedding Rocks.
Elevation change: 200-foot gain, 240-foot loss to Cape Alava.

Approximate hiking time: 4 to 8 hours, depending on speed and destination.
Topo maps: USGS Ozette; Custom Correct *Ozette Beach Loop*.

Finding the trailhead: From Sappho on U.S. Highway 101, drive north on Highway 112 to Clallam Bay and the village of Sekiu. Turn left (south) 2.3 miles west of Sekiu onto Hoko-Ozette Road, which is paved for its 20-mile length. The trailhead is located beside the ranger station at road's end.

The Hike

This trail offers a mid-range day hike to a part of the coast that is inaccessible by car. It receives heavy use due to its ease of access, and a permit reservation system is in place for overnight camping during summertime. Cape Alava is known as a good spot for whale watching, and the mostly boardwalk trail passes a historic homestead site on the way to the coast. The only reliable fresh water along the route is at Cape Alava, and this is stained brown with tannins and should be treated. Wise hikers will bring along an abundant supply of water. Wear soft-soled shoes for traction on the boardwalk.

The trail leaves the Ozette Ranger Station heading west, and a broad bridge soon arches above the sluggish waters of the Ozette River. Soon after entering the forest, the trail branches into two paths. The right fork heads toward Cape Alava and the left fork to Sand Point. Bear right on the Cape

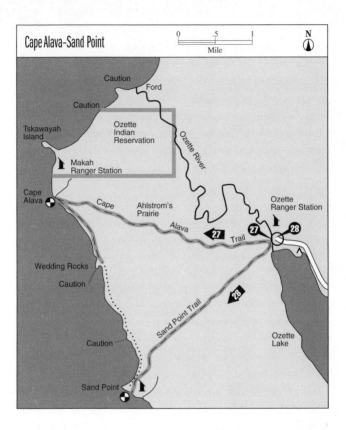

Cape Alava-Sand Point

0 .5 1
Mile

N

Tskawayah Island

Caution
Ford
Caution

Ozette Indian Reservation

Ozette River

Makah Ranger Station

Cape Alava

Cape

Ahlstrom's Prairie

Alava

Trail

27

27

28

Ozette Ranger Station

Wedding Rocks
Caution

28

Sand Point Trail

Caution

Ozette Lake

Sand Point

Alava Trail, which wanders west through young spruce and hemlock underlain by deer fern. The gigantic leaves of skunk cabbage appear in clumps in the boggy pockets of the forest.

The trail soon becomes a boardwalk causeway, which may be quite slippery (especially for hard-soled shoes) during rains. At mile 2.3 the trail passes a rest area that is actually the site of Lars Ahlstrom's barn, long since burned down. The broad stretch of coastal prairie to the west of it is named

Ahlstrom's Prairie in honor of this man, who built the original causeway and was for a time the westernmost homesteader in the United States. A few fruit trees remain to the south of the trail, while the deteriorating buildings of the homestead lie out of sight to the north. This coastal prairie is really a wet bog, filled with sedges, crowberry, and sundew. The sundew is carnivorous: Hairs on the leaves produce droplets of a sticky, sweet-smelling substance that traps ants and flies. After crossing this opening, the trail enters a superb coastal rain forest dominated by Sitka spruce and sword fern.

The trail then descends from the bluff to reach the shoreline at Cape Alava. Upon reaching the cape, visitors are immediately impressed by the collection of large, spruce-encrusted islands that loom offshore. To the north is Tskawayah Island, so close to shore that it can be reached on foot at low tide. This island is part of the Ozette Indian Reservation, and climbing onto it is not permitted. Far to the west, the Bodelteh Islands appear to be a single mass from this vantage point. The long, lean ridge of Ozette Island rises across a rocky tidal flat to the southeast.

Cape Alava is reputed to be one of the best places on the coast to see marine mammals, including the majestic gray whale. This whale is unusual in that it lives on a diet of amphipods that it filters from seafloor sediments. There are campsites among the trees and a tiny creek for fresh water. Campers should be aware that raccoons are particularly persistent pests in this area; keep packs and food out of reach.

The Makah Ranger Station lies a short distance to the north. A Makah village stood here for untold centuries, and a succession of mudslides buried the site from time to time. The slides resulted in one of the most important archaeological digs in North America. The dig site currently contains a laminated magazine article that offers additional information on this historic village site, and artifacts are on display in the museum in Neah Bay. The last permanent residents of this village had departed by 1917, but the Makah still return to the small reservation just to the north on a seasonal basis.

Travelers who seek a longer trek can continue south along a trailless coastal route to reach the Wedding Rocks, a famous site of Makah petroglyphs. To reach the site, turn south, following a narrow strip of gravel that is deep and soft. A rocky shelf borders the beach, and at low tide the numerous tide pools provide windows into the world of sea creatures.

The first headland to be reached is the site of the Wedding Rocks, where a collection of 300-year-old petroglyphs are on boulders above the high-tide mark, clustered in two groups: One group is centered 50 yards to the north of the headland, while the other group is 25 yards southeast of it. There are more than fifty petroglyphs in all, featuring marine mammals, a two-masted sailing bark, and human figures. The most famous petroglyph is the "wedding scene" from which the rocks derive their name. It consists of a male and female figure surrounded by bisected circles, which are a sort of sexual symbol. Carving or defacing the petroglyph site is a federal crime; please report any violations immediately. Turn around here to complete the hike.

Key Points

- **0.0** Ozette Ranger Station. Trail crosses Ozette River.
- **0.2** Trail splits into Sand Point and Cape Alava Trails. Bear right.
- **3.3** Cape Alava. Turn south along the coast.
- **4.3** Wedding Rocks.
- **8.6** Retrace your steps to the ranger station.

28 Sand Point

See map on page 83.
Type of hike: Out-and-back.
Total distance: 6.2 miles round-trip.
Elevation change: 140-foot gain, 180-foot loss.

Approximate hiking time: 3 to 5 hours.
Topo maps: USGS Ozette; Custom Correct *Ozette Beach Loop.*

Finding the trailhead: From Sappho on U.S. Highway 101, drive north on Highway 112 to Clallam Bay and the village of Sekiu. Turn left (south) 2.3 miles west of Sekiu onto Hoko-Ozette Road, which is paved for its 20-mile length. The trailhead is located beside the ranger station at road's end.

The Hike

This route leads from Ozette Lake to the coastline through an old burn in the coastal forest. This path is almost entirely boardwalk and has lots of stairs on it. At the end of the trail is Sand Point, with its sandy beaches strewn with driftwood. Keep an eye out for raccoons, which are particularly abundant around the Sand Point beaches; keep food safely out of reach.

The trail leaves the Ozette Ranger Station heading west, and a broad bridge soon arches above the sluggish waters of the Ozette River. Soon after entering the forest, the trail branches into two paths. The right fork heads toward Cape Alava and the left fork to Sand Point. Turn left as the boardwalk leads into a shady coastal forest of Sitka spruce. The causeway soon breaks out into an old burn that is now a jungle of salal and other shrubs. A few old cedars survived the fire and rise high above the brushy understory. Just before reaching the coast, the boardwalk passes through a narrow band of timber to reach the sea.

The trail emerges at a target just south of Sand Point. True to its name, sandy beaches surround this long spit that juts into the Pacific. There are campsites among the trees to the south of the point, and the acidic waters of a tiny creek provide the only supply of water. Far out to sea, the stately walls of White Rock rise sheer from the open ocean. Cormorants, common murres, and glaucous-winged gulls nest on this isolated stack, and their droppings give the island its white color. To complete the hike, follow the boardwalk back to the trailhead.

Key Points

- **0.0** Ozette Ranger Station. Trail crosses Ozette River.
- **0.2** Trail splits into Sand Point and Cape Alava Trails. Bear left.
- **3.0** Sand Point target.
- **3.1** Sand Point.
- **6.2** Return to Ozette Ranger Station.

29 Hole-in-the-Wall

Type of hike: Out-and-back.
Total distance: 4.6 miles round-trip.
Elevation change: Minimal.

Approximate hiking time: 2 to 3.5 hours.
Topo maps: USGS La Push; Custom Correct *North Olympic Coast.*

Finding the trailhead: From Forks, drive about 1 mile north on U.S. Highway 101 to La Push Road (Highway 110). Turn left (west) and drive 7.6 miles to the fire station. Turn right here on the road to Mora, and continue 4.8 miles to the Rialto Beach Trailhead at road's end.

The Hike

This trip visits a wild and beautiful stretch of coastline at the mouth of the Quillayute River. The coastline to the north is typified by boulder-strewn coves and rocky headlands, but this route covers only the sand and gravel strands of Rialto Beach. Easy access makes Rialto Beach a popular spot with tourists, particularly on weekends.

The trek begins at Rialto Beach, a cobble-strewn strand that extends north for 3 miles. Enormous drift logs have been carried down the river during winter floods, battered and polished by wave action, then heaved high onto the beach by storms. These same winter gales have sculpted Sitka spruce, which crowd the beach in low-growing forms that resemble the krummholz of timberline. A long spit extends south from the mouth of the Quillayute River toward the James Island archipelago. This cluster of islands is guarded by stout, wave-carved cliffs of sandstone topped with spruce

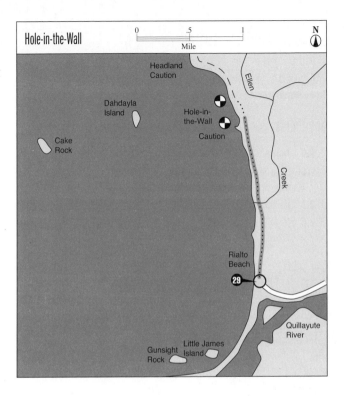

0   .5   1
Mile

N

Headland
Caution

Ellen

Dahdayla
Island

Hole-in-
the-Wall
Caution

Cake
Rock

Creek

Rialto
Beach

29

Quillayute
River

Gunsight
Rock

Little James
Island

and alder. The Quileute tribe once used this cluster of islands
as a natural fortress when fierce bands of Makah swept down
the coast during the course of intertribal warfare.

As the route runs northward, Cake Rock is the major
stack that rises far out to sea, while the more ragged crest of
Dahdayla Island rises from the surf closer to the beach. The
traveling is easy all the way to Hole-in-the-Wall Rock. True
to its name, this minor promontory is pierced by a rounded
aperture worn through the stone by centuries of wave

action. A short trail climbs around the head, which can be passed on the ocean side only at low tides. Travelers seeking a longer hike can continue up the beach for another 0.7 mile before it becomes necessary to begin the hazardous headland crossings. Retrace your steps to complete the hike.

Key Points

0.0   Rialto Beach parking area. Turn north at the shoreline.

1.6   Hole-in-the-Wall. CAUTION: Do not attempt passing around the rock in more than a 5-foot tide.

2.3   Headland. CAUTION: impassable in a tide higher than 5 feet.

4.6   Return to the parking area.

30 The Quillayute Needles

Type of hike: Out-and-back.
Total distance: 4.8 miles round-trip.
Elevation change: 120-foot gain, 200-foot loss.

Approximate hiking time: 3 to 5 hours.
Topo maps: USGS La Push and Quillayute Prairie; Custom Correct *South Olympic Coast*.

Finding the trailhead: From Forks, drive north about 1 mile on U.S. Highway 101 to La Push Road (Highway 110). Turn left (west) and drive 12.7 miles (following signs for La Push) to the well-marked Second Beach Trailhead.

The Hike

This route follows the Second Beach Trail down to a sandy stretch of coastline, offering a day hike or a short overnight trip. This area is known for its diverse tide-pool life. (Feel free

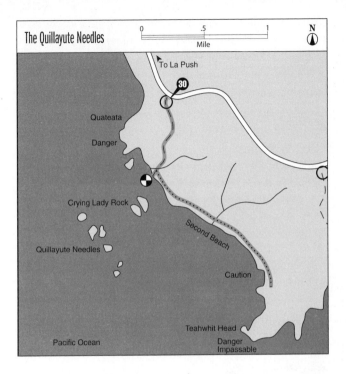

The Quillayute Needles

0   .5   1
Mile

N

To La Push

30

Quateata

Danger

Crying Lady Rock

Quillayute Needles

Second Beach

Caution

Teahwhit Head

Pacific Ocean

Danger
Impassable

to observe, but don't disturb it.) If you plan to travel around any of the headlands here, carry a current tide table and make sure that the critical water level stays lower than the levels noted below in the Key Points when attempting a passage. Territorial disputes between the Quileute people and the U.S. government have closed this trail in recent years; check at the ranger station in Forks for current access status.

The trail begins by winding through a forest of Sitka spruce and western hemlock that sprang up in the aftermath of logging that occurred early in this century. After the trail wanders the wooded blufftop for a time, a wooden boardwalk and steps drop down to the north end of Second Beach. An enormous block of contorted stone named Quateata blocks the northern approaches to the beach, and it is pierced by a natural arch. The Quillayute Needles are scattered across the sparkling waters of the Pacific. This formation is an old wave-cut terrace that has been elevated and weathered into sandstone pillars. Some are massive and stout while others form slender spires.

Turn south and follow the coast as it bends away toward Teahwhit Head. The beach spreads out into a wide stretch of fine sand, raked ceaselessly by turbulent combers. Near its south end, sheer cliffs march down to the water's edge, and tortured stacks stand among the jagged spires of Teahwhit Head. The next headland is trickier to negotiate and can only be crossed during extremely low tides. Beyond it is a secluded cove much like the previous inlet, and a rugged jumble of boulders stretches southwest toward the forbidding and impassable cliffs of Teahwhit Head. Turn around to complete the hike.

Key Points

- **0.0** Second Beach Trailhead.
- **0.7** Trail reaches the beach. Turn south.
- **2.1** Headland. CAUTION: 4-foot tide.
- **2.2** Headland. CAUTION: 1-foot tide.
- **2.4** Teahwhit Head. DANGER: impassable headland.
- **4.8** Return to the trailhead.

31 **Ruby Beach**

Type of hike: Out-and-back.
Total distance: 1.6 miles (round-trip to and from the mouth of Cedar Creek).
Elevation change: 180-foot loss.

Approximate hiking time: 30 to 60 minutes.
Topo maps: USGS Destruction Island; Custom Correct *South Olympic Coast.*

Finding the trailhead: From Kalaloch, drive north on U.S. Highway 101 to the Ruby Beach parking area at mile 164.7.

The Hike

This route leads down to one of the beaches along the southern coast of the Olympic Peninsula, a broad and

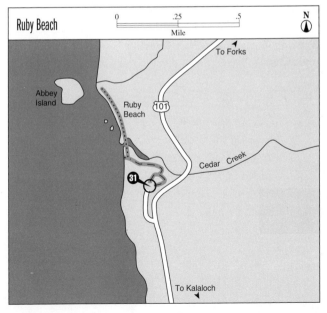

almost unbroken strand that stretches between the Hoh and Queets Rivers. A trail leads down to the beach, at which point day trips of any length can be undertaken. Camping on these beaches is not allowed. Pets, however, are permitted here.

Ruby Beach is known for its pinkish sands, which derive their color from the presence of tiny grains of garnet. Ruby is set apart from the other beaches in the Kalaloch area by the presence of sea stacks at its northern end; Abbey Island is the largest of these. Cedar Creek forms a wide and brackish lagoon near the stacks, and piles of drift logs litter its edges. Destruction Island can be seen far to the southwest. This mighty rock has lived up to its name over the years, being the site of at least five major shipwrecks. Follow the route back to the parking area to complete the hike.

About the Author

Erik Molvar has hiked more than 10,000 miles of trails, from the Arctic Ocean to the Mexican border. Erik has a master's degree in wildlife management from the University of Alaska–Fairbanks, where he performed groundbreaking research on moose in Denali National Park. He currently is director of the Biodiversity Conservation Alliance, one of the West's most effective conservation organizations (www.voiceforthewild.org).

Also by the author:

Hiking the North Cascades
Hiking Olympic National Park
Best Easy Day Hikes: North Cascades
Hiking Glacier and Waterton Lakes National Parks
Best Easy Day Hikes: Glacier and Waterton Lakes National Parks
Hiking Montana's Bob Marshall Wilderness
Hiking Arizona's Cactus Country
Hiking Zion and Bryce Canyon National Parks
Alaska on Foot: Wilderness Techniques for the Far North
Scenic Driving Alaska and the Yukon
Hiking Colorado's Maroon Bells—Snowmass Wilderness
Hiking Wyoming's Cloud Peak Wilderness
Wild Wyoming